87 Things
Teenagers Should Know . . .

Before Leaving Home

87 Things Teenagers Should Know . . . Before Leaving Home

A guide for Young Adults

Lee Burton

Published by Fresh Writer Publishing
1282 N. Van Wert Rd.
Villa Rica, GA 30180
www.WhatYouShouldKnowBooks.com

The author of this book does not give out medical advice or prescribe any forms of treatment for medical, physical, or legal problems. Always seek out the advice of a physician or other competent professional person. The author intends only to offer information of a general nature to help you in your pursuit for emotional and spiritual well-being. You have a constitutional right to use any information in this book for yourself; however the author and the publisher assume no responsibility for your actions.

Library of Congress Cataloging-in-Publication Data
2006938444

Burton, Lee
87 Things Teenagers Should Know Before Leaving Home:

A guide for Young Adults
1. Self-Help 2. Young Adult

ISBN -13: 978-0-9764610-1-2
ISBN -10: 0-9764610-1-3

Printed in the United States of America

The Power of Inspiration . . .

Acknowledgments

First of all, I thank God who gave me the inspiration and the determination to complete this book. I also like to thank those who helped me in my efforts; Tonya Smith for her insightful editorial comments, and Terrell Carter for his final editing. I give thanks also to my mother, Rio, my brothers, Douglas and Raymond, and my son Ian who was much of my inspiration and motivation. I also like to thank my friends and associates: Oliver Johnson, Noel Jones, Christopher Williams, Brian Harris: Blue Box Entertainment, Monica Jones, Ira Wilkins, Hotep: Skinnymen Productions, Patricia Welch, Gary Fields, Coach Alonzo Upshre: Omega Psi, Terry Bolar, Bruce Berry, and Nasr Sonibare.

Thanks to all my nieces, nephews, cousins, and the teenagers who gave me the opportunity to listen and talk to them about life. You all have been instrumental in my motivation for completing the first edition of this book. Thanks again and I wish you all, the best life has to offer.

Contents

INTRODUCTION

To Young Adults...

Finally—you've made it, congratulations! You have finished high school and now you are ready to leave home. So far you have made some "great" decisions in life and still you have many more to make. During the next few years you will encounter countless situations that you have not anticipated. I hope to enlighten you on various topics so you can avoid making some unnecessary mistakes. You are now considered an "Adult," and a lot of responsibilities come with that title. You will encounter all kinds of people in life, and you must learn to recognize the honorable from the dishonorable and the moral from the corrupt.

Although you may not understand your parents completely, remember they are proud of you and they want the best for you.
Think about it . . . Twenty something years ago your parents were exactly where you are now, full of anticipation and uncertainties. Keep in mind; you are the next generation, and during the next thirty-five years or more your decisions will contribute to the direction of all world affairs.

You must position yourself "now" to take advantage of the best possibilities concerning your future. The following 87 Chapters will help you find answers to the many questions you will have in life.

To Parents . . .

As parents we like to think that by the time our children are eighteen years old that we have taught them everything they need to know to make a good go at life. We like to feel that we have instilled in them enough compassion, consideration, integrity, etc. But, the truth of the matter is, a lot of us (parents) have not completely caught up on all those little things we intend to teach our children and make them aware of before it's time for them to leave home. Then before you know it, they are on their way out the door, ready to explore a new life. They are done with high school and on their way to college, the military, or the wedding chapel. You might want to say . . . "hold up" wait a minute; I still have a lot of things to say to you! I forgot to warn you about this—and we haven't discuss that yet. But, there will always be things you want to emphasize even though you know you can't always be around. For a few years, your children will separate themselves from you; but the older they get, the more they will confide in your knowledge.

I have also included in this book several blank pages for you to write down some of your own personal advice. The 87 Chapters are intended to cover the most important issues your teenager will face once they have moved away from home.

No matter how excited your child is to be out on their own, most young adults will experience some form of anxiety when they actually move away from home. There is a certain amount of fear that lurks in the back of their mind, along with unanswered questions. They will have uncertainties and insecurities while becoming fully responsible for themselves.

This convenient handbook of information is designed to help them over a few hurdles and hopefully keep them headed in the right direction for making the best choices in life.

Advice

When taking advice from someone, listen carefully to what is being said. They may not live in a million dollar home or drive the most expensive vehicle or wear the latest in name brand clothing, but that does not mean that they do not have some good solid advice to offer. There is something to learn from nearly everyone. People you encounter in your day-to-day life have a lot to teach you as well as the well known authors and public speakers. So don't look at the common person with the pre-judgment that because they don't have a lot of material things that they don't have good advice to offer you. Even so-called "unsuccessful or unaccomplished" people can teach you valuable lessons. Even if it's how *not* to make the same mistakes they have made. Listen and find out why they don't feel as successful as they would like to be. They will tell you about their mistakes; use this information so you won't make the same mistakes. Those who have made mistakes wish they could change them . . . but most likely can't un-do what is already done; they may want to inform you so you won't make the same mistakes. If it seems to make sense . . . latch on to it, it's probably advice worth taking.

Most older people want the best for you and want to help you along life's journey. But, there are some "bitter" older people who's paths you will cross that are angry about their choices and disappointed with their lives. And you will sense their bitterness and feel the tension in the air when you are around them. Just remember . . . , you can "learn" something from anyone!

Anger

Everyone gets angry at some point in life. Whether it is provoked or not you should always struggle to maintain your control and restrain yourself from anger before it leads to violence. Never allow anyone to make you so angry that you are "out of control."

When you let Anger take Control:

1. **Anger** will cause you to say or do something you will later regret when you act on a spontaneous reflex and not on logical thoughts.

2. **Anger** makes you unable to think straight, you can't concentrate on the real situation at hand. Stop and think . . . why is this person trying to provoke me to anger? Yes, they want to see you act out of control. Why satisfy them by giving them the desired reaction they were hoping for?

3. **Anger** will cause you to lose time, sometimes hours or days replaying the incident in your head when you could be doing something productive or having fun.

4. **Anger** can cause you to wind up accidentally hurting or killing an innocent bystander.

5. **Anger** can cause you to lose your job or the respect of someone you care about.

Anger has landed many young adults in prison just because they *failed* to control it. Don't let old stupid slogans or myths and foolish people anger you. People will sometimes lie on you or make up stories about you . . . yet; you should not respond by acting ridiculous along with them. It usually turns out to be disastrous in the end.

Excessive anger is self-destructive and it is most likely caused by some form of stress in your life. You must identify your stress and find a positive and effective way to get rid of it. Try writing out your thoughts and doing some kind of physical exercise to relieve you of your stress. Counseling and reading self-help books can help too.

Answering Questions

This pertains to people you are not sure of, such as: strangers, suspicious people and associates.
As a precaution: Never answer a question . . . UNLESS you know "WHY" the question is being asked!

If you are suspicious of someone, you may want to consider answering their question with a question. For instance, when confronted with a question by someone you do not trust, politely ask them "why they are asking that question . . ." Then the person will tell you why they asked you the question. However, if they get angry because you are answering their question with a question, then they probably have deceptive motives. You have no obligation to a stranger. It's ok to say NO to someone you do not trust! Never feel obligated to do anything if you don't feel it is safe.

Because you are a young adult, there will be all kinds of people asking you questions and some questions you should not answer. Always have a stock answer for the people you feel you do not trust.

For example if you are driving and stop at the gas station—a stranger walks up to you and asks you, "which direction are you going in?" Ask them why they want to know. Then they will say something like . . .they needed a ride in the direction that you are going, or they just wanted to let you know the traffic is pilled up on a certain highway.

Remember, they may be testing you or sizing you up to take advantage of you or try to sell you something. If you know the purpose behind the question—then you will be better prepared on how to answer it. If the stranger decides to ask you for a ride, now you can easily refuse by saying I'm going in the opposite direction, or I 'm not comfortable with giving you a ride. Predators, Desperados and Con-artists come in all kinds of clothing and they can be any gender.

Apologies

Apologizing for something is not the easiest thing in the world to do. It's even more difficult if your closest role models in your life such as your "parents" never apologized to you for anything while they were raising you. In this case it becomes something weird to you and makes you feel quite uncomfortable when you want to apologize for something.

Why Apologize?

Here are some reasons you may want to apologize to someone.

1. Because you have wronged someone and you know it will make them feel better.

2. You were partially or totally at fault.

3. To keep the incident from being on your conscience for several weeks, or longer.

"Never" apologizing in life implies that you are never wrong. Remember it's only human to make mistakes. We all do!

Note:
An apology doesn't have to be verbal, it can be sent in a card, an e-mail or a letter. Besides, it's worth the relief you will feel afterwards. Free your conscious and feel free to *Apologize!*

Arguments with Friends

How do you handle an argument with a friend? Very carefully. Just because they are a friend, it doesn't mean that they must agree with you all the time.

A good friend will . . .

- Point out potential flaws in your personality, so you can work on improving them.
- Lift you up and bring out the good in you.
- Debate with you on different subjects and "brainstorm" for new ideas and solutions.
- Help you avoid trouble.
- Listen to your complaints and be a shoulder to cry on "sometimes."
- Comfort you when you are depressed.

Also, a friendship should not end just because you totally disagree with each other on a few subjects. No two people agree 100% about everything. And a friend that agrees with you "no matter what" is not a true friend. Sometimes it is ok for a friend to set you straight on certain situations. But a good friend will do it in a loving considerate sort of way. Right or wrong friends will overlook certain flaws in each other. And, friends shouldn't stay mad at each other for several weeks or expect gifts to be given back whenever you disagree about something.

Most people have very few "real" friends.

Articulation

Being able to clearly express your ideas and feelings are extremely important. Poor articulation can make communication very confusing; so remember to be specific and use names whenever possible.

For instance: He told him to go over there to see him and after that she told him to get back in his car. Is this three or four different people? How many people are we talking about? If you don't use names or (proper nouns) who's to know "who in the heck" you are talking about? Be more specific and descriptive when explaining a situation or discussing a matter.

It is very frustrating trying to figure out what someone is saying. Even more importantly you can find yourself in a lot of trouble if someone misunderstands or misinterprets what you intended to say. Because no one is a mind reader, communicate carefully and say what you mean and mean what you say. Don't get frustrated if it does not come out right the first time, just say that's not what I meant to say— it came out all wrong— let me start over. Be as articulate as you can when explaining something.

Body Language

Your body language is like the cover of a book. In an instant, people will read you and come to a conclusion about who you are and what you will become. People are very judgmental and you probably are too! When you see someone on the street that looks very different or "unusual" you make a conclusion that they are some kind of weird freak or something, don't you? The way you walk, talk, dress, wear your hair, sit, stand, and smell are all indicators of what people will think of you. People young and old will categorize you. They will sum you up in about ten seconds! Do you walk with your head down, do you walk slow like you have no place to go, do you look people in the eye when they are talking to you? What image are you trying to portray, good, tough, shy, responsible or polite?

> How do you want to be perceived? If you don't care how you look, no one else will either and you will be overlooked because you appear not to care about yourself.
> However, if you care about how you present yourself, others will care about you too.

When you are on your own and are entering the job market, you will more than likely have to make some adjustments to how you dress and communicate. It's okay to act a little different at work, most people "Act" a little different at work than they do at home. Actors get into character all the time, and then they get paid-- go home and be their typical selves. News Reporters, Public Speakers and Lawyers all get into character too so they can deliver their message clearly and effectively. I'm sure they don't talk the same way at home. Never worry about those folks that call you phony, they probably don't have much going on in their lives anyway. Besides adopting a slightly different character is not being phony, most of us have slightly different personalities that bend and sway a bit depending on our environment. You "should" act a little different in a sweat suit than you do in a business suit. Keep in mind, you are not being phony, you are simply tweaking your personality a bit to be more suitable for a certain career position. So, get into character for that important job so you can get top pay!

Boredom

A lazy mind becomes bored quickly. Boredom is a frame of mind that "you" are mostly responsible for. You should not rely on everyone else to entertain you. You will have to figure out how to entertain your own mind. Some people constantly say they are bored. The problem is that they just haven't learned to use their imagination to keep them occupied.

How to keep from being bored?

First of all, you should have something planned to do everyday. If your daily plan is always the same, then make some changes to your leisure time. One or two days each week, plan something different. Do something different every other weekend. Hang-out with different friends or associates . . . the ones that are doing something positive and unlike the ordinary. There are too many things going on in the world to let life become tedious.

Books are an excellent way to escape and have vicarious experiences. Browse the shelves at a bookstore and see what sparks your interest. You may be surprised to find a hidden interest. You can also rent a couple of books from the library. Take a look in your local news paper and sign up for a craft class or become a member of a sports club. There are too many positive activities to get involved in to be bored. What do you think people did for entertainment up until the year of 1898 when radio was invented—and television wasn't even around yet.

Bullies

When you graduate, you will have gotten rid of "some" of the bullies in your life. However, once you get in the big world you will still encounter bullies. Only now they could take the form of a boss or a co-worker. If this is the case, you can take your complaints to someone superior in the company. You can use the chain of command or bypass it if you have reason to. You can also file a civil complaint.

Another approach to resolving an issue with a bully is: to slowly try to make friends with the hopes that if they get to know you maybe they won't act so hostile towards you. This sometimes works, but not always. Sometimes nothing works, not even your complaints to higher ups and you just have to go to a new job to get them out of your hair. But if you do choose to leave, it is a good idea to let other employees whom you can trust know why you are leaving. They may be having the same problem with the same person and if enough of you have the same legitimate complaint, eventually something may be done about the intimidating person. An organization you can contact for harassment on the job is the EEOC (Equal Employment Opportunity Commission).

On the flip side, you should never bully anyone either. When you say hurtful things to someone . . . you can <u>not</u> take spoken words back! That person has to repeatedly feel the pain of those hurtful words for months or sometimes years. Some people are more sensitive than others and will always remember the emotional pain that hurtful words or actions can cause.
A Bullies main objective is to emotionally control and demean you with verbal insults and constant demands.

Camping Safety

Those of you who grew up camping and still have a passion for it may want to go camping after you leave home. But I warn you . . . camping can be a dangerous adventure for anyone, especially young adults.

<u>Things to consider when going camping:</u>

1. Female campers always consider taking a male with you. Females out camping are targets for predators.
2. Camp in a well-known safe site; stay away from the primitive campsites. Camping on the weekends is usually safer because there are more people around.
3. A Hunting knife or mace can provide some protection.
4. Let family or trusted friends know when and where you are going and when you will be back.
5. Take a cell phone with you even if it's prepaid.
6. Don't drink alcohol, especially if it's against the law for that camp site. Drinking will keep you off-guard, making you more relaxed than usual and more vulnerable.
7. Remember campfires can spread in a "few seconds." Never walk away from a simmering ash, pour water on it and around it before you leave the area.
8. Be friendly but not too friendly with other campers. They may be sizing you up to take advantage of you.
9. When hiking, never tell suspicious strangers where your site is . . . find out where they are so you can visit them if that is the case, or you can meet at a certain public spot at a certain time on the camp site.
10. Take an emergency kit for bug bites, snakes bites, bee stings and poison ivory.

Always be prepared !

Caution!

Be cautious of people who "give" too much.

Trust no one 100%, remember most people will not give you much of anything for "free" unless it's a family member. But still always be cautious about taking too much of anything from anyone. If you accept too much money, clothes, favors, etc. from someone . . . you are in their debt. You will owe them something, or at least this is what they will "set you up" to believe. They will want you to feel as though you must *repay* them in some kind of way. **They may want the following favors from you:**

– Sexual favors

Male or Female, homosexual or heterosexual; their objective may be to get small or large sexual favors from you. Small sex favors will eventually turn into greater demands.

– Transporting favors

Be suspicious of someone asking you to take a bag or package some place for them. You never know what could be in it! You could be transporting drugs, weapons or something illegal. Also, never steal information for someone, even if you are in a position to easily acquire it. Be careful giving associates or strangers a ride in your vehicle, you never know what they might be caring on them. Never risk doing something illegal or immoral.

– Delivery favors

Gossip, Lies, or Half-Truths; they may implant a lie or some gossip in your head anticipating that you will go an repeat it to cause friction between others. Never allow someone to use you as a messenger to irritate and confuse others.
(See: Modeling or Older Acquaintances)

Chemicals

From the time you wake up, go to work or school, and back home, you will have been exposed to over fifty different kinds of chemicals. Chemicals such as the ones found in: cosmetics, detergents, insecticides, pesticides, pet treatments, paint, dry cleaning, plastics, and various cleaning agents used at your job or school.

Cosmetic chemicals are found in: deodorant, shower gels, soaps, mouthwash, skin make-up, hair shampoo, perfume, hair dyes, and sanitary products. And harmful chemicals used in and around the house for maintaining the home are: kitchen cleaning products, air fresheners, pesticides, synthetic carpets, upholstery, varnishes, paints, glues and vinyl flooring. When there are an excessive amount of electrical appliances in your bedroom it's known as, volatile organic chemicals (VOC's).

Try to avoid as may "chemicals" as possible. You could start by: using organic products, minimizing dry-cleaning, avoiding the use of pesticides in your home and opening your windows for fresh air instead of using synthetic air fresheners.

Chemicals in H_2O

Some common chemicals used in your drinking water to kill germs are: chlorine, chlorine Dioxide and Chloramines, which are used to help disinfect drinking water. When they are added to the water they react with the naturally occurring organic matter that is already in water. Even these chemicals which were chosen by municipalities to clean and purify your drinking water they have some adverse effects on the body.

Other organic and chemical contaminants found in drinking water are: Pesticides, Herbicides, Arsenic, Asbestos, Aluminum, Fluoride, Barium, Copper, Lead, Mercury, Nitrate/Nitrogen, Selenium and Thallium.

Many contaminants are not filtered out in the cleaning process. And they will enter your body and disrupt and impair the body's natural chemical balance by weakening the immune system. You can help your body avoid many of these chemical contaminants by not drinking tap water from the faucet. Instead drink "Natural Spring Water" or "Distilled Water" which is less stressful to your kidneys.

(See: "processed food" for chemicals in food)

Church Religion

There are so many different kinds of religions in this world, and as the years pass there are even more being formed. Some of us were raised in a religious environment and some of us not. Some people don't believe in "God" and we call them atheist. However, most people believe that there is a God or a "Supreme Being" and something much more superior to mankind. Somehow we were created, so there is definitely a supreme being; man has proven himself incapable of re-creating another human being. Their attempts at cloning, still requires taking the cells of an already existing creature to duplicate. So with that reality, we know there is a "Master Creator." It doesn't matter whether you were raised Catholic—Baptist—Muslim or one of the other hundreds of religions; we all have primarily the same struggles and desires.

Knocking someone else's faith or beliefs is never wise. You may not know the history behind their religion and your current religion may even be a spin-off from what theirs once was in some distant past. If you have not studied their faith or religion, try not to judge others and especially do not judge a person in a negative way because of this difference. They were taught by their parents to believe as they do, just as you were. Think about it! Once you discover the complete meaning behind their faith, who knows you may even change your mind about your own beliefs. As a young adult, your faith "is" what your parents taught you; what you learned as a child, not what you have decided on your own. You were lead into your beliefs and did not have a choice in the matter. So how would you know what to believe unless you have studied in-depth the concepts and origin of other faiths.

In other words, if you have never studied for YOURSELF the foundation of various “Religions” how could you know the true essence of it! Be careful of what you know . . .

Quote-

"I think we ought always to entertain our opinions with some measure of doubt. I shouldn't wish people dogmatically to believe any philosophy, not even mine."

Bertrand Russell
British author, mathematician, & philosopher (1872 - 1970)

Cleaning

By now you've heard the saying "Cleanliness is next to Godliness," I say, Cleanliness helps you stay disease free.

Most germs are transmitted through the air or from touching objects. Wash your hands frequently; four or more times a day. Sometimes it is a good idea to wash your hands "before" you use the restroom, but always wash them thoroughly after you use it. Wash them several times while you are cooking, and "always" whenever you walk into the house.

Bacteria and intestinal parasite eggs can easily enter your body a number of ways and cause severe damage to your insides. Change your kitchen towels frequently and your bathroom towels too. Cleaning the inside of your car often will help keep away germs too. So "clean" the germs away . . . because they won't disappear on their own.

Keeping your apartment clean will make you feel better about yourself and others will see that you are not a *slob*. No one wants to live with or visit a messy person, male or female. If your home is nasty and disorganized, chances are your business environment is hectic and chaotic too. It is harder to feel organized when your daily environment is messy. So, impress "yourself," get organized and clean up after yourself!

What is the difference between a **"Neat Freak"** and a **"Clean Freak"?**

Neat Freaks . . .

Neat freaks like things to "appear" clean but they are not necessarily clean. They don't mind tossing things into a closet or cabinets as long as the clutter is out of sight. Their homes usually "appear" to be clean at first sight. But if you look closer you will discover that their toilets are dirty, the edges of their floors and baseboards are filthy, and their dishwashers are full of dirty dishes. So—things are not always what they seem, a "Neat Freak" is not necessarily a "Clean Freak."

Clean Freaks . . .

What a "Clean Freak" wants is cleanliness! "Germ free" and sterilized! They can "also" be neat freaks. But on the contrary, a "Neat Freak" may not be a "Clean Freak. A "Clean Freaks" primary concern is to make sure the germs are gone. A "Clean Freak" may tolerate a little more clutter than a "Neat Freak" simply because they know that their floors, toilets, showers, dishwasher and refrigerators are clean and germ free.

Also, "Clean Freaks" are more likely to use cleaning agents such as bleach, pine-soil and alcohol a whole lot more than a "Neat Freak." "Clean Freaks" are less likely to have roaches in their home because they will make sure the bugs won't have any crumbs to feed on. Whereas "Neat Freaks" are only concerned with the way things "look" not how clean they actually are.

Areas that most people fail to keep clean:

1. The entire toilet, especially the front part, just above where your toes are when you are standing in front of it; a perfect habitat for feeding germs and bugs.
2. Mirrors, Dresser tops, fan blades, window blinds, T.V. and computer screens; they collect dust often.
3. Floors, especially the kitchen and bathroom floors. Sometimes a mop just won't do. You may need to kneel or squat

and use a rag and bucket to really get the floors clean. Disinfectant soap or isopropyl alcohol can work in place of some popular household cleaners. Always have a decent vacuum, the carpet holds tons of dust that can give you allergies and in some cases bronchitis or asthma.

4. Every night your skin sheds dead cells that bedbugs and mites feed on. You should change your linen once a week and especially after heavy sweating.

5. Trash-cans carry tremendous amounts of germs. Clean them inside and out regularly.

Your mother won't be there to ride your back about keeping your living space clean. But her message is this . . . invisible germs and bacteria breaks down your immune system, which lowers your resistance and contributes to the cause of you getting sick.

College or not?

Should it be "your" choice? Some young adults choose College; some choose the military or trade school. Which ever one you choose, ultimately you should have the final decision. But I warn you. Never make a decision just to be spiteful. Research both options before making a final decision, remember it's "your" future that is at stake!

"Parents know best" . . . well usually they do, but they can't give you the motivation to do your best in a career choice that "they" have chosen for you. If your choice turns out to be a mistake, then that is the choice that you will live with. Parents sincerely want the best for you but they do not always know what your inner passions and desires are. You can only be motivated if you are doing what "you" think is best for you.

Again, you should never refuse to do what your parents ask of you regarding you career and education just to be hostile, it may come back to haunt you in your future life. Try not to do the opposite of what they say just to be rebellious. Always consider what they have to say and weigh the benefits regarding "your" future. Because, what you should really be concerned about is your future . . . and you don't have time to waste! Before you know it, you'll be thirty years old and wondering where did all the years go. Just ask anybody that is over thirty, see what they say.

Do your homework and find out what the pay scales are for different kinds of occupations You have to decide if this is the income class you will be comfortable with. Not every one is interested in becoming a Doctor, Lawyer, Airline Pilot, or top

Executive. But, if you desire comfort and like to travel and have the finer things in life, selecting a career that pays at least $65,000 may not be a bad idea. And if you are thinking about becoming an entrepreneur, remember, you must first be well educated in a certain field for a *period* of time before you really "know" about that particular industry. Nearly every industry requires some kind of degree to earn above average income.

(Also see: Entrepreneur)

UPBEAT
STAR
HOT
better
So crafty. So versatile
ONE OF A KIND
IMPORTANT
creative
POPULAR
Outstanding
"WOW" Factor
BEST
IN
Ultimate
Inspired
advanced
professional
EXCLUSIVE
100%
SMART
Quality

Confidence

Everyone likes to feel confident in everything they do. True confidence is usually something that is acquired over a period of time. For example; being confident in a new job may take a few weeks or a few months. And if the job is difficult it may even take a few years to develop an adequate degree of confidence. What makes a person confident is, **"KNOWING."** Knowing your job—knowing your presentation—knowing your capabilities and knowing your disadvantages. When you are well informed, well studied, well skilled and well practiced, you are more comfortable and therefore more confident. When you are knowledgeable you are less intimidated by others and more confident in yourself.

Knowing your own shortcomings and accepting them is a part of achieving confidence too. Accepting that you are not perfect and no one else is either.

Remember;
EVERYONE has faults and a few flaws should not dampen your confidence. When you are comfortable with yourself, others will recognize this and trust and admire you more when this level of self-acceptance is reached. However, confidence is not arrogance or self-conceit and there is no need to be arrogant in order to radiate confidence.

Consideration

Consideration is a very important quality to have in your character. Although some people are lacking in this area, most people have a reasonable amount of it. However, consideration as a young adult sometimes is challenging. Why? because you are more concerned with yourself during your young adult years. However, you should not treat other people in a rude or thoughtless manner, this includes your parents. Consideration at home and with family is equally important and everyone should take into account a certain level of consideration throughout their entire lives.

One especially important thing to take into "consideration" is; "your parents pocket-book." Using a credit card, a check book, or a banking account without permission is an extreme demonstration of outright inconsideration! Always think about how you would feel if it were done to you by your children!

And remember, thoughtfulness towards others of all races is also an important element for being a considerate person. Consideration makes the world a more peaceful place.

Remember to be considerate in how you treat others!

Cooking

Although you may not be able to cook like a Chef; by the time you are eighteen years old you should be able to prepare several simple dishes on your own. Like scrambling eggs, cooking grits or oatmeal, baking a potato, cooking macaroni, making pancakes, steaming fresh vegetables and baking fish or chicken, just to name a few.

Don't rely on someone to cook for you all the time. Everyone knows that eating fast food every day is not a healthy source of nutrition for the body. You could find monthly recipes and weekly tips just by watching some of the food preparation channels such as:

[Food TV Personalities]

Nathalie Dupree "Grand Dame" of Southern cuisine
Mollie Katzen: Vegetarian cuisine
Graham Kerr: the Galloping Gourmet
Emeril Lagasse: Creole and Cajun chefs: Emeril Live!
Martin Yan: Yan Can Cook and the Best of China
Garvin on HBO
The Barefoot Contessa on the FOOD channel

Consider purchasing a simple cookbook from the bookstore or ask your mother, aunts, or cousins to write down some of their recipes and mail them to you. But don't expect to get their "secret" ones though . . . everyone has a few secret recipes that they won't share with anyone. When they mail them to you, keep them in a special folder in the kitchen where you can find them just when you need them. Keep their telephone number next to their recipes just in case you need to call them and ask a question. Also, the internet can help you find recipes. If you search around I'm sure you could find web sites offering free recipes to download.

Remember, fast foods will feed the hunger in your tummy but it is not what the body needs on a daily basis. You will need to eat more junk food just to try and feed the body all of the nutrition it needs, whereas a good home cooked meals contains more nutrition in smaller portions. When your body doesn't get the proper nutrition, it will crave more food . . . trying to squeeze out some nutrition just to feed its cells. Subsequently this will cause you to over eat and create fat cells that lead to overweight.

Avoid cross-contamination by washing your hands frequently while you are cooking especially when handling meats. Never eat out of the same plate that had raw meat in it without washing it first; this is a sure way to get salmonella poisoning. Also eating raw eggs could cause salmonella poisoning. Always take food out of the can before storing it in the refrigerator to prevent contamination.

Always remember, a properly prepared home cooked meal is a better choice for you body than fast food. When cooking, try to minimize your butter, margarine, salt and white sugar; they prevent the body from functioning at its maximum capacity.

Ice carries unhealthy bacteria and food left out of the refrigerator two hours or more starts to grow bad bacteria that tax your immune system.

(See: Nutrition)

Co-workers

Co-workers-

Should you get involved (intimately) with co-workers or someone that live in your neighborhood? Usually getting involved with co-workers is not the brightest thing one can do, even if it's a boss. So what happens if things don't work out after six months or a year? What kind of predicament will that put you in. Will you feel uneasy or angry if they dump you? How about if you dump them? How will this affect your performance at work and how will it make you feel when you have to look at them everyday? The tension could be unbearable.

Some people can do this successfully, but most people can not for any long period of time. And rarely does this type of arrangement work out. So if you think there aren't any negative consequences for going out on this limb, go for it. But make sure you ask yourself some hard questions first!

Neighbors-

Also, weigh the consequences of dating someone that lives in the same apartment complex as you. Always consider the future of the relationship, what if it does not work out eight months down the road. Moving is an option for some people but not for everyone for various reasons. You might want to consider "passing" on this idea too . . . think long and carefully about it first.

Credit Cards

Credits cards are fairly easy to get . . . but hard to get rid of and they carry a "huge" responsibility. The credit card companies' objectives are designed to let you create tremendous amounts of "debt," that way they can keep you financially obligated at a super high interest rate for several years.

You probably already have one or two credit cards or at least know a few friends that do. However, just because you can acquire one does not mean that you really need one. The sooner you learn to budget your money without using a credit card, the better off you will be in your financial future. Most young adults are up to their ears in credit card debt before they reach their 28th birthday. For most people it's easier to over spend with fake paper than it is with real cash. It's very easy to say . . . "oh, I will pay for it later," this is very unrealistic unless you have plenty of loot in the bank. Why is this unrealistic? Because . . . "unexpected bills" are always popping up and you will always "want" more stuff!

*** * * Don't expect your parents to pay your debts. * * ***

It is i-n-c-o-n-s-i-d-e-r-a-t-e and thoughtless. So before you spend too much, maybe you should consider cutting up the credit card(s) that you now have and pay them off completely. A lot of people get credit cards to build up their credit, which is fine, if you can control your spending. Never max out your credit card(s), it will be torture trying to get that balance down to ($0.00), not to mention that you won't get any big scores from lenders for maxing them out either.

Over 1.5 million people file for bankruptcy each year, and it's getting harder to file for Bankruptcy because of new laws and regulations. Besides, a bankruptcy stays on your credit report for 7 to 10 years. Think about your student loans if you have any and think about your future salary. How long will it take you to pay-off those creditors?

Five years? Seven years? You should stop and seriously consider the long term effects that a negative credit card will have on your future. Requesting a credit card involves nearly as much thinking as making a career choice . . . so never get overly excited about having one and don't take spending "plastic" too lightly.

Probably the best advice regarding preserving your credit is to never sign up for a consumer credit card until you have plenty of cash stacked in the bank. And if you do get one, never max it out and make sure you pay it off at least every six months. Otherwise having one will probably do more damage than good in a long run.

Beware! It is one of the fastest ways to damage your credit score! Also, you should never accumulate debt with the intentions of filing for bankruptcy; it could get you into trouble with the reviewers. If you do manage to damage your credit, you will have a hard time getting a car, computer, apartment or home in your name. Also, many employees now require that you have "decent credit" before they will hire you. Remember, keep a positive credit history, *never* let anyone use your credit card and don't leave it out where someone can steal it. Always be hesitant to use a credit card, instead use cash if you can. Do not let your desire for "Things You Don't Need" get the best of you!

Also, be careful about those credit card offers sent through your email or slow mail, vital information can be stolen in a number of ways. You can get your name taken off of their mass list of pre-approved credit offers by calling the "opt-out" phone line at: 1-888-5-OPTOUT (1-888-567-8688).

Dating

There are a lot of different combinations of dating going on these days however, this sections refers to boyfriend and girlfriend as in heterosexual dating. First you have to decide if you want a serious relationship or a casual relationship. If it's a casual dating scene that you seek, then you should also make sure the person(s) you are dating are aware of your intentions. **Never mislead anyone by letting them think that they are the only one that you are seeing**. And never get involved with someone who is not yet divorced.

Casual dating is all about "getting to know" different people without making a decision to commit to one person. You are saying that you do not want any ties or demands made on you at this time in your life. You want to share their company but you don't want a commitment. When you are young it is hard to know exactly what kind of man or woman you genuinely desire or what kind of companion you will be compatible with. After dating a few people you can make a better decision about what kind of person you really want to settle down with.

Well let's just do a quick view of **Serious dating**. Serious dating is when you are looking for a deep commitment and long term relationship; it's a whole different ball game. To sum it up, in short, you want a mate that you are most compatible with. You don't want to get hitched up with someone based on superficial stuff; like how good they look. The physical body will change in time, so don't get all hung up on that. Then there is "the money thing," you don't want to get caught up with someone just because their pockets are deep or they have a V.I.P status . . . you still have to spend a lot of time with this person. Also, you should not get caught up with someone just because they are a challenge and you're out for the quest. Healthy relationships aren't just about conquering; instead, analyze whether you really like the person and listen to your own intuition to decide if the feelings are mutual. Finally, **do not base your whole relationship on sex.** If you only get along in the bedroom and no where else, you are probably not really compatible with each other. This is a good indication that there isn't enough balance to endure a lasting relationship.

Is it Love, or is it Lust?

(See: Relationships, Marriage)

Death

There is always "fear" in the unknown. And we fear the most simplest of things, like spiders, cockroaches and mice. Just as this is a learned fear from our parents and friends, so is death from our forefathers and ancestors. Once you "accept" that death is the flip side of living, it will be much easier to accept and understand. We are all going to die— someday.

There is an old saying, "fear not the dead but the living; they are the ones who can hurt you." Some people are afraid of dead bodies at funeral homes and grave yards. Dead is dead and there is not a breath of life in the dead. Many believe that the same entity that created you will be the same entity whose arms you will walk into when you die. Hummmm . . . there are probably some stipulations to it— probably based on how you lived your life?

Non-the-less, death of a relative is very very painful. You will miss their presence, and thoughts of them will be with you for as long as you live. But bear in mind that they are no longer burdened with the worries and pressures on this earth; they will go to their rightful place. Don't worry about death, it will come at the appointed time for each of us and try not to morn indefinitely for the dead. They would want you to get on with your life and be the best person you can be. But most of all, try not to be depressed or feel guilty for a long period of time. Negative emotions can manifest within the body ruining your health and make you physically ill.

"The fear of death follows from the fear of life. A man who lives fully is prepared to die at any time." ~Mark Twain

Depression

We all experience a certain amount of depression at some point in our lives. The most common reasons are related to; career disappointment, relationship problems or health issues. Depression can also be brought on because someone special in your life has died.

What ever the reason, no one wants to endure depression. It is one of the "worst" experiences we will have in our life time. Most of the time it is a temporary condition and can last a few weeks. But for some it can last several years. If you have been depressed for several weeks you should seek professional counseling immediately to help make your life more bearable. You may feel that no one around you can truly relate to how you are feeling and that you are in a sinkhole all by yourself. You may feel a hollowness inside yourself, a void that you can not explain or do not understand. These are normal feeling of depression but they will disappear in time.

Try to be "HOPEFUL" because, in time things will get better! You can't help but feel rotten when you are the one stuck in the mud. It might take a while but, you will get through it. You may feel like hibernating or at least not socialize for a while, just remember it is a temporary condition and it won't last forever. Try reading some literature on the subject of "coming out of depression," or go online for a depression screening test. Remember, you will *grow* stronger once you have made-up your mind to move on to the next phase of your life!

Divorce

Whether your parents are already divorced or in the process of divorce, understand that it is not your fault. You are not the problem! It is because of their relationship. You are not at fault here.

Adults who have lived together for several years experience all sorts of issues that sometimes cannot be worked out between them; isn't it possible that you may also experience similar problems in your marriage in the future? Hopefully you will find a better solution to your problems. But for now, never feel like you are the cause of your parents divorce, it's just not true. You may not understand why two people who were so in love and devoted in the past, now can't seem to work out their differences. Because you may not have a "complete" picture of what is actually going on, try not to judge your parents for their decision. So, don't hold grudges and don't judge at this time, no matter which parent is your favorite. "You Won't Have All the Facts" that brought your parents to a divorce. What you see and understand as a young adult may change when you are older.

Quote-

"You are young, my son, and, as the years go by, time will change and even reverse many of your present opinions. Refrain therefore awhile from setting yourself up as a judge of the highest matters."

Plato, Dialogues, Theatetus
Greek author & philosopher in Athens (427 BC - 347 BC)

Drugs & Driving

The leading causes of death for 15 to 24 year olds are automobile crashes, homicides and suicides. Alcohol is the primary fact.

Why take the chance . . . a drink and a drive could set you back about $3,000 in fines, penalties and a damaged driving record. Ask yourself-- is it worth it?

Always establish a designated driver or plan to take a taxi home when you go out with friends. Remember drinking and driving does not mix and there are thousands of young adults killed in drinking and driving accidents each year in the USA.

Mixing cannabis and other drugs impairs your judgment tremendously. SO . . . , if you do not want serious fines and penalties . . . AND if you don't want to wake up in another world, Think before you Drink!

Always drink **"less"** than you can handle and you will always stay in control of yourself. Alcohol beverages suppresses your inhibitions and may cause you to do something stupid, not to mention it might cost someone their life. Practice being <u>stubborn</u> when it "helps" you, but not when it "hurts" you.

Remember:

- While impaired, your reaction time is much much slower.
- Look both ways before pulling out into traffic from a traffic light, never assume that on-coming traffic will stop when the light changes.
- Use your peripheral vision, some accidents are prevented by seeing a vehicle out of the corner of your eye.
- Anticipate what other drivers might do, they may not see

you. Observe traffic further than two vehicles in front of you. Never "tailgate" or follow too closely.

- Avoid driving behind vehicles caring things that can fall on to the road.
- Blowing your vehicle horn can sometimes prevent an accident for you *or* another driver.
- Vehicle maintenance is very important, brakes and good tires especially.
- Hydroplaning is not a myth. You can not steer a vehicle when it's floating on water. Drive slower on wet surfaces.
- Keep a spare vehicle key hidden some where outside of your vehicle for emergencies.
- Headlights should be on from sun-down to sun-up. You want other cars to easily see you.
- Be especially careful of vehicles "pulled over" on the side of the road and change lanes if you can.
- Never change lanes while going through an intersection!
- Remember, most medications do not mix well with liquor.

The law says you must be 21 to drink, this is for a reason. Inexperienced driving mixed with alcohol is a recipe for disaster.

Ignore peer pressure!

"Think" of some ways to avoid peer pressure "before" you are confronted with it.

Embarrassment

Everyone gets embarrassed at least once, and some of us a few times within a life time. What embarrasses us at age fourteen will be different at twenty-seven and still different at thirty-seven and so on. The older we get, the things that embarrasses us will change. Sometimes you can't prevent being embarrassed; it happens to the best of us. If there is nothing to learn form an embarrassing situation . . . then try hard to forget about it. It will be less painful in a few weeks, just try not to take it too seriously.

Things that embarrass you while you are young are:

-That science project that went wrong when you were in front of the class doing a presentation.
-That verbal tongue lashing your mamma gave you right in front of your friends.
-When and adult caught you in a compromising situation.

Those are a few embarrassing situations you may have found yourself in when you were younger. It doesn't always end there. Now whether you're in college, the military, or on the job; in day to day life you will at some point be embarrassed again. Sometimes it can be avoided by envisioning an upcoming situation or preparing for the unexpected. But then again, sometimes you cannot avoid it. It may happen by accident or because of your own carelessness.

When you are older, embarrassments can include "life achievements" based on society standards. For example; when older people feel they have not accomplished enough in life, they can be burdened by embarrassing feelings because they have not achieved as much as they thought they would in life.

If you are feeling self-conscious about your short comings, the best thing to do is start working on improving yourself. But you must question yourself thoroughly to see what it is that is most important to you in life. We weren't all put on this earth to accomplish the exact same things. So, find out what your strong points are and work towards developing your best talents. Once you have mastered a talent you should never feel embarrassed about it. Be content within yourself and not worried about living up to someone else's standards. Be thankful to be able to do something pretty good. Be happy with who "YOU" are.

There is an old saying . . . "you can't please all the people all the time . . ." so just worry about pleasing yourself!

Emergency Situations

You should think about the possibility of an emergency situation and how you would handle it.

What would you do?

You just seen a car run off the Interstate and crash into a tree and you are the only one around, what would you do?

- What if you are at home watching T.V. and someone breaks-in on you. What would you do?
- On your way home, what if you notice that someone is following behind you. What would you do?
- What if you saw a pedestrian get hit by a vehicle and the vehicle just kept on going. What would you do?
- What if you were out with a friend and they got drunk but insisted on driving home. What would you do?
- What if you seen a three year old child walking down the street alone at 2:00 a.m.. What would you do?

Although some situations are so bizarre and you could never foresee it in a million years, some situations you can have a plan already somewhere in the back of your mind of what you intend to do if caught in that particular situation. However, if you are too shaken-up, you may not think of your "plan of action" immediately, but if you already thought of one, it is more likely to pop in your mind than if you had not thought of what to do already. Believe it or not, you will have a few emergency situations in your lifetime. Try to be prepared . . .

Entrepreneur

Now-a-days everyone wants to become an entrepreneur. Well . . . everyone is not entrepreneur material. Not everyone has the discipline and expertise to set-up and run their own business. Some of us need traditional jobs. You have to make an honest decision if you can be an entrepreneur or not. Can you endure the possibility that there may be times where you can't make ends meet? What will you do? Being your own boss is a tough road but you can be successful at it if you have; an "in demand market" and if you are determined and skilled in your field. When you sit and visualize about all of the good stuff that goes along with independence, don't forget to envision the down side and the possibility that things could go wrong.

It is documented proof that most businesses fail within the first two years and the few that survive usually go through a tough time for a few years. So if you have a product or service in demand and you are skilled and knowledgeable about it, you may want to take the chance. But, it is a tough road and many are defeated before they become successful.

A good way to tell if you would make a good entrepreneur is, think about when you were younger, were you always trying to make money and were you good at coming up with creative ideas to make money? If so, you probably have the determination to take on this kind of venture. On the other hand, if you waited on your allowance or begged your parents for money all the time and never went out and hustled to earn your own, you are probably not entrepreneur minded. Be truthful with yourself. Some people are comfortable being an employee and are not interested in the burdens of becoming an entrepreneur.

If you are not sure about becoming an entrepreneur, then find employment in the field that you are interested in and learn all about it until you are very skilled in that occupation. By doing this you are also learning discipline and are acquiring good work habits which are "imperative" if you wish to become an entrepreneur. Then later you may want to consider going into business for yourself. This is a good way of learning the skills of becoming an entrepreneur. Pick up a copy of Entrepreneur Magazines and see what interests you.

Failure

We all have expectations for ourselves; we also have the burden of expectations from others and sometimes feel obligated to live up to them. Choosing which expectation to be most concerned with can be complicated. Just remember, when you are young your parents are trying to mold you into respectable adults according to society standards and according to what they have learned in their lifetime. But you have your own mind, and you want to make your own choices.

Young or old we all have failed in something in life. If you do not try your hand at whatever you feel you are capable of doing —you won't ever know what kind of abilities you have. But failure is not a dirty word. All humans fail, there are small things we fail at and there are larger things we fail at. But no matter what you fail to do or accomplish, there is always something that you will be successful at doing. However, if you set you goals too high without putting in the necessary work, you are guaranteed to fail. To be successful in something you must first become proficient in that particular field of study.

Sometimes you may fall short . . . and give up on your goal and then there is a certain degree of shame in failing to live up to your "own" expectations. Or, you just might change your mind. Do not accept anyone telling you that you are a failure. Ultimately you are here to live up to your own expectations and no one else's. Failure and success is determined by each individual.

Remember, if someone taps you on the shoulder and says "you aren't doing to well" and asks if you want some advice, you just might want to listen to them and weigh the facts to see if what they are saying makes sense or not. Many people set goals in life and never accomplish them. Sometimes their goals aren't practical, such as, "I want to become President of the United States" but they hate to study government, politics or world studies. Chances are this is an impractical goal, so don't set your self up for failure.

But don't worry too much about failures; we will all have some if we ever dare to dream. Some reach their goals and some don't, all you can do is try. And if it doesn't work out, pat yourself on the back for the effort you put into it. Many people won't even try or make an attempt at anything.

"There's not a human on this earth who has not felt the misery of failure, unless their only desire was to wake up and drift through the day without any expectations in life."

"FEAR"

What to do with it . . .

We all have fears; we fear leaving home, we fear leaving our friends, we fear people not liking us, and we fear not accomplishing our goals.

Sometimes life experiences will help create certain fears. But mostly we allow ourselves to create our own fears. Fear can cause us to stumble, and it can also keep us from trying. And it can even keep us awake at night, which can cause our bodies to eventually become ill.

However, you can get rid of many fears if you try hard enough. The sooner you realize that fear is the flip side of courage, you can start working on minimizing your fears. Fear also has its benefits. It has been known to get your adrenaline flowing and help you react in certain circumstances, and it usually lets you know when a situation is out of your control prompting you to move on . . .

Just remember, never let "Fear" control you —you control it! *Never let it paralyze* you or cause you to think irrational. Use your willpower to fight off the anxieties inside of you.

First Impressions

First impressions are very important. When a person sees you for the first time they instantly get and idea about who you are. They speculate what you are about, and what your perceptions are regarding life. All within a few seconds they will sum you up!

People will quickly form an opinion about you without knowing you at all. Call it fault by human nature people assume things based on what has been taught to them through generations and so forth.

As a result, you will be judged by adults and your peers according to how you dress, what your hair looks like, your skin, your facial expressions, and even the way you walk. You will judge others too. Young people have a tendency to think that older people are slow, drab, stuck in the past and archaic in their thinking. When many older people are a lot faster than one could ever imagine . . . once you get to know them.

So we all pass judgment, it's just going to happen. So then, seriously consider how you want to *affect* others. If you are going for a job interview, how do you want to be received? Excessive self-expression can be left for when you are not at work. The world is a stage and you have to know exactly what costume to wear for whatever part you are performing. You may have to speak a little louder, a little slower, and a little more articulately. Know what "character" you should be in at all times. To an extent, we all have a number of subtle personalities. You act a little different around your friends than when you are around your parents, don't you? So be yourself and get "in character" for the appropriate places.

Fitness

When you see a "fit" person what do you think? I don't mean a body prepared for a bodybuilding competition or someone who looks anorexic; just a person who looks like they take care of themselves. You know they probably eat right or at least their diet consists of more good food than bad. They feel pretty good about themselves don't they. And they usually have plenty of energy, yes? And they resemble "good health" don't they?

So . . . , if you want this for yourself then you have to exercise at least three or more days a week. That does not necessarily mean going to the gym. You could go skating, dancing, or swimming. Maybe some tennis or some other kind of sport that makes you sweat. If your metabolism stays up, you are unlikely to become overweight. Most people especially young people are not too happy with being overweight. If you feel that you are overweight you might want to consult a doctor and trainer to get yourself into shape. Most people find it hard to work-out and stay on a fitness program own their own. Some people start working out with a friend . . . and then a few weeks later, their friend quits the workout program. If this is the case, you should still continue on your workout program. Do it for yourself! You will feel better about "you" in the long run. Don't say -- oh well I will wait until I'm older to start working out. You must do it while you are young if you want to maintain a healthy body when you are older. If you don't create good muscle tone when you are young, chances are you will never be able to once you are older.

Listen to this . . . If your "body" has ever been in shape before (hopefully like now while you are young) it is more likely to be able to recall the fitness level of when you were fit. In other words, a person who was fit when they were young will find it easier to keep their body in check when they are older. It's called "muscle memory." Look at it this way, a person who never introduced themselves to physical fitness when they were younger will have a hard time getting into shape when they are older; so all the more reason to get fit while you are young.

Females have a lot more body fat than males, and after giving birth it is a lot harder to get back into the shape you were in before pregnancy. However, it you were "fit" prior to pregnancy it's easier to get back into shape. Remember there are a lot of husbands and wives complaining about how their spouses just let themselves go after they got married. Again, what you do to your body in your youth, will REFLECT in your body when you get older, and that's a FACT! So don't neglect your body, stay in shape and eat the right foods. Limit your fast food restaurant visits to twice a month and workout a three times a week. Join a work-out facility or buy a manual treadmill. Your body will thank you for it when you are older.

In a nutshell . . .

Most illness are triggered from poor diet, poor nutrition and a lack of exercise. What you eat in your youth and how you exercise, will help determine your health when you are older and possibly how long you will live.

Keep a full size mirror and a scale in your bathroom, this will help your subconscious control your urge to over eat.

(See: Nutrition)

FREE

The word "Free" does NOT mean "Free" anymore! The definition of free is: Something available without charge.

You may see products or services advertised on T.V. or on the radio saying it is ABSOLUTELY FREE just call the toll-free number. However, what this usually means is -- they will send you their product "if" key word (if) you order the complete set or sign up for twelve months, or if you agree to a reoccurring monthly bill for a particular product or service. There will be some kind of terms and condition you must agree to in order to receive their so called "free" product or service.

Whatever it is that the advertiser says is Free, it is NOT free! There is a catch and they will want your credit card number too. You had better listen carefully or read the "membership agreement" or "purchase agreement" carefully, or you might be paying several months for something you thought you would be getting for free. Don't pay them and they will slap that delinquency on your credit report with a quickness! Many times a company will say something is free for 15 days and then start automatically deducting lumps of money each month out of your account.

Remember, nothin' in this world is "Free" anymore "not-a-thing." The word "FREE" was diluted, altered and transformed back in the 1970's. Nobody gives away anything free anymore, now, everybody wants to get paid for barely giving you anything. Sellers want to hook and real-you-in so they can get into your pockets and spend your money—that is the bottom line! Most of them don't really care if a product is useful or even if it works well.

Also, if someone makes you an offer and you don't "get" it? then Forget it! If it doesn't make sense what someone is asking you to invest in, then leave it alone, no matter how good the deal may sound. You can bet . . . , if it is a "paid" advertisement, it is a lure to get you to "buy" something!

Friends, Acquaintances or Associates?

When you leave high school you will lose lots of friends and acquaintances. Many of them will relocate to different states for college or the military. In your life time at least "one" of your friends or acquaintances will deceive you. You won't see it coming but chances are it will happen before you are twenty five years old. They will set you up, tell a lie on you, talk about you behind your back, or trick you into doing something wrong. They may even go as far as to have intimate dealings with your boyfriend or girlfriend.

Choose your friends carefully!

Sometimes you will catch yourself saying "my friend" and they are only an acquaintance. An acquaintance is someone you hardly know. Be cautious of what kind of information you share with an acquaintance or an associate. You never know who might deceive you. An acquaintance could care less about your feelings; they hardly have an obligation to you. Even friends are sometimes jealous of one another in some way or another and this envy could one day get the best of them. There is not a lot you can do about that. Forgive them and move on. But never let someone deceive you twice.

Associates are people you may see on a regular basis but they are not necessarily a friend. They have less emotional ties to you than close friends. They can make your life fun, or difficult. Sometimes co-workers turn into friends and sometimes a relationship develops "only" because you see them five days a week. And under other circumstances you may not even get along with this person. None-the-less you shouldn't trust them with all your personal information. Ask yourself . . . would you still be friends with this person if you were not working together? Certain things in your personal life should not be shared with co-workers, period!

Always put the people in your life into a particular category so you know how to relate to them, as "Friends," "Associates," or "Acquaintances." Friends are people you tell some of your deepest secrets to "and" you know some of their deepest secrets too. Never tell someone everything about you, when they haven't told you anything about themselves. If you are a big talker that's fine, but you should also know how to be quiet for a while, listen and ask questions too. Friends listen to each other; one person should not dominate all of the conversations.

Gay, Choice

Some people are born homosexual (gay) because of their altered sex chromosomes and some are gay merely by choice. If you are born that way and want to change it, you can pray and or rely on doctors and medicine.

However, we know that everyone who claim to be homosexual were not all born that way. So let's talk about "gay by choice" which seems to be more prevalent in today's Gay society.

Gay people come in all different races and forms as you are aware of by now, and according to the laws of this land, homosexuals deserve to be treated as human beings and given the same respect as all persons. You can be prosecuted for any negative actions motivated by disliking gay people. Still, many people are homophobic and loathe the gay population.

Many gays fall into the gay world through curiosity and experimentation. And some are introduced into gay activity at a very young age. But some homosexuals do not decide to acknowledge their sexual preference until they are well past their thirties.

For a moment, set aside any spiritual beliefs you may have about homosexuality; just consider the "procreative" reproductive make up of your physical body. You know that two humans or two animals of the same sex, can not, has not, and will not ever reproduce!

And, human genital manipulation can alter the exterior, but it doesn't alter the internal composition of a person. We were made different for a reason . . . hummm, perhaps to be able to reproduce.

Even if you have experimented at a early age with a partner of the same sex, this <u>does not</u> necessarily make you gay, it just means that you have been exposed to a different kind of behavior. If you were molested at an early age by an older person of the same sex, this does not make you gay either. If an older person took sexual advantage of you, do not fault yourself for that. Whether they were the same sex or opposite sex; it was absolutely wrong!!! Studies show that this kind of abuse can be perpetual and many times those who molest have also been molested at a young age. Although this does not excuse them in any way, it is sometimes the case with many sex offenders.

Again, whether you are male or female, if you were sexually abused by a person of the same sex, you shouldn't feel like you are homosexual just because you were coerced into participating in this activity. Instead, be confident that you can have a typical heterosexual relationship if you choose to. Most people make a choice to be gay. But, you have to decide if this is right or wrong according to your moral and ethical beliefs. A child's mind is impressionable and can be made to believe that many things are acceptable; which can be confusing later in life.

You may feel somewhat bisexual because of certain experiences, but you have to go with what your soul tells you is right or wrong and not just your physical body.

Remember:

> The body may want to do drugs, over indulge in liquor or have promiscuous sex with strangers. But just because the body craves these things . . . does it make it right, safe, or rewarding?

Gossip . . .

Gossip is: Casual conversation or unconfirmed hearsay about other people, mostly offensive and insulting; a person who likes talking about other people's private lives.

Gossip is one of the most demoralizing things a person can do to damage the reputation and respect of someone. It can be dangerous and can get you into a lot of trouble. Just look at the

rag papers sold in the grocery stores like the National Enquirer, Star Magazine, and Globe. All these papers are based on gossip. It is sad that people like to hear a bunch of crap that isn't even true about other people.

Never gossip about others; it is not honorable and you will eventually get gossiped about too if you stay in the perimeters of a group of people that entertain themselves by constantly having negative things to say about others. Beside, people who spend a lot of time gossiping about others usually have no life of their own. They are bored with who they are and need to absorb themselves deep into other people lives to make themselves feel important. If you are busy studying, learning, accomplishing and advancing yourself and working to improve who you are . . . you will never have time to waste on extensive gossiping about others.

If you didn't see it with your own eyes, or hear it from a reliable source, and then you go repeat what you heard —what does this make you? Remember, gossip can do a lot of emotional damage to a person once they find out about it. Never spread lies about people. You wouldn't want it done to you, would you?

Grocery Shopping

Five things to remember about grocery shopping:

1. Never go grocery shopping when you are hungry. Eat First! Before you walk into the grocery store make sure you are not hungry, otherwise you will be buying all kinds of stuff you really don't need. Everything looks and smells good when you are hungry!

2. Plan you meals for the week. Make a list of things that can make a complete meal. What will you need to prepare the dishes that you are planning to make?

3. Stick to the list and don't add other things as you shop. Avoid impulsive buying.

4. Think of what meals you can make that will last two or more days. Chili, lasagna, soups, stews, beans and rice, etc. Think about it; two fast food meals total $10.00; instead you could prepare a meal that will last three or four days for the same amount.

5. Compare the cost of the brand names or try a different brand that's cheaper it could save on your grand total. Experiment a little, but do not try too many unfamiliar brand names at one time. Some brands vary a lot on flavor but some taste just about the same.

Also, keep a note pad in the kitchen so when you run out of something you can make a quick note of it. And don't forget your list the next time your go to the grocery store.

Try to limit grocery shopping to once a week or every two weeks. The more you go the store the more you will spend. Stay on budget. Only spend what you have in your grocery budget to spend. Always tally-up what you have in your shopping cart before going to the register. Most grocery store items are between $1.00 and $4.00. Touch each product and add it up by placing them to one side. Keep aside the item that you may not have enough for and put them on the counter last. Tell the cashier you are not sure if you have enough for the last two items.

Always look for the expiration date on meat and dairy products. Also, if there is no visible price shown for a product, do not put that product in your cart. Most likely it will cost much more than you want to pay. Compare the product prices for different sizes and brands and calculate the unit price against the package price. Watch the scanner when checking out to make sure the right price is rung up. Mistakes can happen especially if an item is supposed to be on sale. Use coupons if you don't mind clipping them, they can be a big help when money is tight.

Guilt

Broadly speaking, we will all experience guilt at some point in life. There will be "something" that will cause us to feel the shame of guilt. It may be a small offense or a larger crime of some sort.

However, you should never feel guilty for leaving home if you are of age and you are ready to move on to experience life. Many parents find it hard to let go of their children and let them make their own decisions. But how else will you learn and experience life for yourself. After 18 years of caring for you, it is sometimes hard for parents to say good-by to the ties they have had over you for so long. But once you are 18 years old, in this country you are pretty much considered an adult. Except for the "catch 22" —you can't drink liquor until you are 21. Just commit a crime and see if they'll put you in juvenile detention; "nope" you are guaranteed to wind up in an adult jail facility. You are adult enough to even join the Military . . . but no drinking. The old double standards, you are not old enough to make crucial decisions, nor are you old enough to drink liquor, but if you commit a crime you are certain to be charged as an adult. The world is full of catch 22's. Get ready for the Catch 22's you will hear for not getting hired right out of High School.

Anyway, it's your life, and you shouldn't feel guilty about the career choice you have made. Although your parents may be more experienced in life, **"you" have to live with the choices you make!** Weigh the differences, ask others for their opinion, and make sure you are not choosing a career just to make them angry . . . it may backfire on you! Maybe your parents are not aware of your genuine interests and true talents. They may want you to choose a career that they have always wanted for themselves but did not consider your strong talents including what excites you and what motivates you.

Make your career choice based on very sound decisions not hostility or resentment. And never let anyone put you on a "guilt trip" once you have made up your mind.

Also, there are those few people who will try to make you feel guilty just to gain control over you. If you are not sure about your feelings of guilt about something, go ask someone you can confide in. Find someone you feel that is a truly fair person, possibly an older person. Ask them for their opinion about whatever it is that you are feeling. Listen carefully; they probably can help you resolve what's going on in your head.

Helping Others

Helping others is usually a good thing, but sometimes not. If it's costing you way too much of your time and you can't get the things done that you need to, then you are spending too much time helping others. However, most people don't help out as much as they can; some for fear that they may be taken advantage of or thought of as being weak.

Holding a door open, giving directions, holding the elevator, bringing someone a snack, letting someone in front of you in traffic are all small daily acts of kindness. Every act of kindness increases the endorphin in your brain helping you to feel happier. This usually causes the person you were kind to to do something kind for some one else. It works in the opposite way too. Sometimes when people are mean to us for no reason, in return we are a little mean to the next person just because it has put us in a negative mood.

Never let someone dull your spirits for the day; brush-off your clothes or create some kind of jester for yourself to use whenever you encounter someone that is angry about something in their life and takes it out on you. The jester you create is simply a way of brushing off the bad vibes they sent your way.

A benevolent spirit is contagious, so help out when you can. If you see someone scuffling and you can make a situation easier for them, why not help; provided it's safe. You shouldn't volunteer your help merely based on their race, creed, age or weight. Even though there will be days when you are angry at the world and you won't lift a finger to help anyone. Just remember it is a passing emotion, so don't stay stuck in that negative mode for too long, it could become a part of your personality.

Holiday Spending

Christmas, New Years, Valentines Day, Birthdays, Weddings, Graduations, Traveling, Vacations.

One of the **biggest** mistakes people make during the holidays is . . . spending too much on gifts.
If you have not budgeted or saved for the occasion, do not put yourself into debt to purchase gifts or to travel. Try not to borrow from family and friends. Borrowing money is "Not" a good practice! Using credit cards is borrowing, except they carry very high interest rates and penalties if not paid on time; Instead of borrowing try saving up for those special occasions.

Spending $500.00 on gifts and then not being able to pay your rent doesn't make good sense. If traveling is not in your budget, then send your gift through the mail early enough to get to its destination on time. Be creative, unique and practical gifts are always remembered.

If you plan on going out to party for the holidays, don't spend the utility bill money, you will regret it later. Find someplace to party that doesn't have a cover charge. Or you can give a party at home and have friends bring their own food and drinks. Never go into debt because of the holidays. It is not worth six months of trying to catch up with your bills. Make a budget and stick to it! If $200.00 is all you have to spend for the holidays and you see something you like for yourself, put it on lay-a-way or if you put it in the cart you can take it out of the shopping cart at the last minute. Is the item a "want" or is it a "need." When shopping for others you will always see something you desire for yourself. But use strict discipline and ignore your wants for a few weeks and stick to that financial budget so you won't regret over spending. Also, if you buy small gifts two or three months prior to the occasion, you won't feel the pinch as much.

Homesick

Being homesick is a symptom that nearly everyone goes through. Some people go through it earlier in life, some go through it later. Some people never stop going through it and some never feel homesick and are too happy to be away from their families. But, if you are feeling homesick and distance is an major issue, the only thing you can do is stay in contact with your family by telephone, e-mails or slow mail.

Make friends with people around you, they can help take your mind off of far away family members. If you can, make plans a month ahead of time to be with your family and friends during the holidays. If not, if you're the type to stay on the telephone for hours, call them at the most cost effective time of the day. Some young adults have a stuffed animal as a companion to keep them company and to keep them from feeling lonely. As the years go by and the older you get, you won't feel homesick as much, especially after you make friends with some of the young adults in the area.

Suggestions:

Make friends; get involved in activities with **positive** groups of people. Don't be a cling-on, have courage. Your parents are afraid for you but . . . at the same time they feel they have given you the basic tools for life and secretly they are eager to see how well you will use them.

You are going to miss your family and friends at home. After all that is a part of growing up. And for a while, you will have uncertainties and fears while becoming independent. You will feel all alone at times, it is only natural, but, it will help you grow as a person. However, if you really truly feel you need to go back home for another year until you have grown-up some more, call home and talk to your parents about how you are feeling. They may have some noteworthy advice for you.

Hurting Others

Being insensitive and hurting others is very unfair and it is also dangerous too. Never direct your physical anger towards someone. Practice getting in touch with your emotions. If you are feeling frustrated or irritated about something, lie down and think; try to figure out exactly what it is that you are "actually" angry about. This will help you understand yourself more as a person. Try to see yourself through the eyes of other people. Try to put yourself in someone else's shoes and see if you can relate to what they may be feeling. Think about what has happen in the past (recently or several years ago) that could be angering you. Maybe someone said something to you and you wish you had responded differently, or you may have made a mistake and are angry with yourself. Maybe you have some resentment for this person from years ago. What ever it is, think hard and long about why you are upset. Try hard to understand exactly where your hostile feelings are coming from.

Never lash out or attack someone (verbally or physically) just because you feel like it. No matter who it is, it is bad communication. Whenever a person feels attacked, they will close their mind to any logical communication and they will lash back at you. Remember, never deliberately hurt someone. Think of how it would feel if it were done to you. "Hear" what you are saying when you are talking and always be aware of how the other person is receiving what you are saying. No matter how subtle, people will react somehow to what has affected them. Some peoples emotions are more delicate than others. Find out how to recognize various forms of body language. Practice this old saying- "do onto others as you would have them do unto you."

On the other hand; if someone has hurt you deliberately or indirectly through their actions or verbal attacks . . . You might want to confront them! You must decide if it is worth it, but never confront an angry or hostile person. Everyone has a conscious and once you let them know in a dignified way that they have hurt you, their conscious will be affected and most likely they will try to make amends for it. Usually, once you "call them out" or "confront them," their attitude will change. Just like the devious kid in school who always did unscrupulous things behind the teachers back. Once she confronted the kid, the bad behavior eventually stopped . . . unless they had some deep-seated behavior issues; it's pretty much the same with adults.

However, if you have tried a few practical approaches to get someone to stop treating you unfairly and these attempts have proved unsuccessful, then you should consider ignoring or avoiding this person. Most likely they don't have much of a conscious and have chosen to live their life recklessly.

Hygiene

It's been said that a smelly person is the last to know that they have B.O. (Body Odor).
Usually you are the LAST person who can smell "you." Body odors can come from your hair, scalp, ears, nose, mouth, underarms, genitals, anus or feet. All of these areas are important to keep clean on a daily basis, otherwise they will create odors.
Some "Males" seem to think that because they don't have a "Vagina" (which can harbor more bacteria), that they don't need to clean their genitals as thoroughly or as frequently as females do. If you are one of those who think this way, you are dead wrong! Males can also accumulate odors from moisture and sweat a few hours after bathing just like females.

In other words, male or female, you may be the last person who will smell "you" when you are "funky." Usually others will smell you long before you smell you, unless you have a really sensitive nose. So clean your body's "five points" thoroughly, and daily. Always use a TOWEL. Don't be disillusioned; your hands will not do a proper job of cleaning, if they did, the invention of the small face towel would have disappeared hundreds of years ago. And you must put some effort into rubbing these areas with soap and water. Merely dragging the towel over your body won't get rid of the dead skin and sweat that causes odors.

"Five Points" are: Mouth, Under-arms, Genitals, Anus, and Feet.

Clean behind your ears and inside of them, wash your hair every day or if your scalp is dry at least once a week. Remember ear wax stinks; toe jam stinks, and skin folds and creases collect bacteria which stink. Gargle and brush your teeth three times a day; morning, noon and night. You may not be able to smell your breath but others will certainly smell it. Most females shave their under-arm hair, but both males and females should consider trimming genital hair about once a year. Odor can permeate the hair in these moist areas. If you wear gold caps, crowns, or braces on your teeth you will need to take "extra" care to insure good hygiene.

Poor hygiene can keep you from getting employment, keep you from getting a companion, and it could make people not like being around you. You don't want everyone to run when they see you coming.

Not brushing and flossing regularly can cause gum disease, tooth decay and bad breath. In some cases chlorophyll capsules will help to reduce bad breath that comes from the stomach. See your dentist about tooth decay and gum disease.

Also, if you have "crater tonsils" which can cause halitosis (*bad breath)* you might want to consider having your tonsils removed to eliminate the bad smell that's caused by food and bacteria getting packed into a small cavity in the tonsils.

Remember, when you **"Burps"** it usually stinks almost as bad as a fart, so blow them out your mouth in a direction that won't be offensive to anyone. Always gargle in the morning, floss your teeth daily and never wear your socks or underwear twice without washing them. Many kinds of fungus grow in soiled clothing. Flushing the toilet several times while having a BM will keep the toilet from clogging. And always wipe until tissue is clean; use a flushable wet-wipe if necessary.

Most people do not have "Perfect Hygiene" 100% of the time —unless they are obsessed with cleanliness and taking three to four showers a day. You don't have to go to that extreme, but you should make an effort to maintain good daily hygiene habits.

Excessive body order may be an indication of bad bacteria or parasites in the body. This can be fixed with three or more weeks of body cleansing with an "Herbal Cleanse" and a fruit and vegetable diet.

Integrity

Be honest, truthful and sincere. Have principles of right and wrong behavior.

By now as a young adult you should have developed a certain amount of integrity. Your parents taught you right from wrong; they taught you to obey the laws of the land and not to rebel against the basic standards of society. Like; don't lie, don't steal and don't cheat. And some of our parents taught us the Christian Ten Commandments. Exodus 20.

In essence what they were teaching us is to have "integrity." By being honest and moral you have a better chance of living a long happy and successful life; although, there are people without much integrity that have material wealth and a simulation of happiness which was acquired by lying and cheating others. But are they genuinely happy?

To be genuinely happy and content with your accomplishments in life, always have integrity in all of your dealings; whether you are dealing with the rich or poor, young or old, male or female, black or white. Nothing good ever comes from bad. Bad choices pull you down, and good choices lift you up. Remember never be so selfish and greedy for power or money that you would manipulate or deceive someone to acquire it.

"Always do the Right Thing."

Internet Dating

Since the boom of the Computer age there are literally hundreds of internet dating sites, and their population is increasing by the years. You can find heterosexual, homosexual, interracial, sado-masochist etc. It's all there if you are looking for it. Depending on the site, it usually costs about $20.00 a month and must be paid by automatic withdrawal through your bank account. This is an alternative way to meet and date people in your age group. You can see their picture, read their profile and get a general idea about what they are looking for in a mate. You can also exchange mail-messages through the site, and if you both are interested you can set up a date to meet each other.

This can be a good way of meeting people although there is potential danger in this kind of dating if you aren't careful. You should not automatically trust what a person says through email or through a few telephone conversations. They may not be telling you the God honest truth. People can disguise themselves and give you wrong information about themselves, and sometimes it takes a while to honestly know what their intentions are. They could be someone who is planning to hurt you, or they could be an older person trying to manipulate you.

-Things to Remember

Whenever you set up a date with someone, always meet them in a public place and at a reasonable time of day. A date between 10:00p.m. and 8:00 a.m. is "NOT" the most reasonable time of day to meet someone. Consider meeting in public where there are lots of people around, such as, an arcade, a restaurant or a grocery store. You should wait until you are totally comfortable with that person before you let them come to your home or give them your home phone number. Anyone can do a reverse phone number search to get the address to where you live, so it's better to only give out your cell number. Use your common sense and keep in mind that you don't really know this person at all. Talk to your friends about them and pass on information or even forward some of their email sent to you to a close friend. All you know about them is what they have told you. It takes "time" to get to know someone. Females should especially find out all you can about males you've met on an internet dating site before getting too comfortable with them. You might even consider taking a good friend along with you on a first date, such as a double date.

Although, you may not have heard many horror stories about internet dating and think that it's all good . . . it's because, a lot of people just won't report something that they are embarrassed to talk about. So be safe and don't be too secretive about meeting up with strangers. Don't think because you are a male that a trick can't be played on you. Always play it safe!

Jails & Prison

"Crimes for Money" or "Crimes of Passion"

"Most" people are in prison for either . . . crimes for money, or crimes of passion.

Never commit a crime, don't talk about committing a crime, and never let anyone talk you into committing a crime. It's a well known fact that a high percentage of African American males between the ages of 19 to 29 are either in jail, in prison, on parole or on probation. Check with the Bureau of Justice Statistics for more detailed information on incarceration. Do not become a victim of this statistic!

"Jails" are locally operated correctional facilities that confine persons before or after a judgment and having a sentence of one year or less. A *"Prison"* is operated by the State or Federal Government for someone sentenced to one year or more and usually convicted of a felony.

Remember, if you visit other countries; make it your business to know what their laws are in that country. Some things that are permissible in the United States are crimes in other countries and hold severe punishment. Do some research on whatever country you plan to visit. Several cases have been reported about young adults visiting other countries only to find out the hard way that certain behaviors aren't acceptable in that country. It is very hard to get out of prison in a foreign country. Some of their laws are very extreme and very different from those in the United States. You may find that their punishment does not fit the crime at-all in comparison to that of the United States. Also remember that even in the U.S.A. Laws vary from one State to another.

Hopefully you will never find yourself in such a situation, however, if you require a lawyer, know that most lawyers specialize in a certain matters.

A Criminal Defense Attorney will handle all criminal charges such as: Sex Offense, Drugs, Domestic Violence, Theft, and Fraud. "Criminal Court" is a court having jurisdiction over criminal cases

A Civil Defense Attorney most likely will handle cases such as: Divorce, Corporate Law, most Auto Accidents, Wills, Probate, Insurance claims, certain Death claims, Medical Malpractice, Personal Injury, and Bankruptcy.

Never commit a "Crime of Passion" against a relative or friend. Don't do it! Leave, walk away or move to another state if you have to. Sometime it's just better to put miles between you if you can't live peacefully with someone. Just because they are your relative, it doesn't mean that you will automatically like each other. Sometimes "space" helps people to heal and deal with

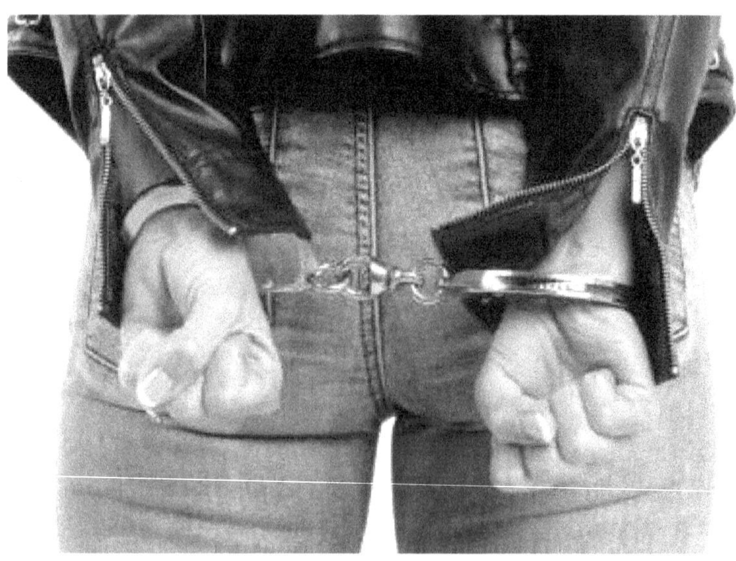

their hostilities. No one wants to be manipulated, aggravated, or told what to do.

Never commit a "Crime of Passion" against a Lover. **No, you don't have the right to hurt someone, just because they no longer want you involved in their life.** In time you will get through the tough times after breaking up with your lover. It's okay to love someone, but to try and "possess" them is not wise and will only lead to trouble. Think about it. Would you want someone to try to make you love them? Stop! Think about your future! Remember, there is life after losing the love of your life, but it's going to take a while to get over it. Everyone has to get over someone in life and sometimes more than once. Everyone hates rejection, but sometimes we must accept it gracefully!

(See: Role Models)

Jealousy

Jealousy is by far one the most "intense" emotional vibrations you will ever experience as a human being. Animals also experience jealousy too, but let's just discuss human jealousy. That horrible feeling that seeps way down into your gut and spreads throughout your soul, and surfaces as a fierce anger eager to strike out at what ever or whom ever has caused it.

Whether it's jealousy over a sexual rival or jealousy over someone else's achievements, it doesn't feel good when you are experiencing it. At the end of jealousy there we are; no matter how painful it is, it confronts us with our own deepest fears and anxieties!

You must try very, very, very hard to "control" your jealousy. Never let it get the best of you; it can cause you to do some pretty stupid things, some you may regret. Remember you can not control others no matter how much you may love them. You can not control their heart, their feelings, or their actions. Talk to several older people about their jealous experiences and see what "set backs" it caused them.

And if you are jealous and envious of what others have, then work harder to master your own talents —then you can appreciate your accomplishments and also others. In this day and age every one wants to "own things," but you must do the ground work to get you to that level. But still, there will always be someone who has more than someone else.

(See: Wounded Hearts)

Jobs 35k or 65k

Many entrepreneurial lectures start off with the phrase; "what -is -a -Job" what does that mean? Then they will tell you, a JOB stands for— "**J**ust **O**ver **B**roke" and so on . . . .

In essence they are right. In today's economic society if you aren't making at least $35,000 a year you will be in the hustling scuffling class. That's right "scuffling" just to buy groceries, maintain a vehicle, pay utility bills and keep a roof over you head every month. Hardly anything will be left after paying basic monthly expenses. What about a savings account or miscellaneous "fun" money, or how about those emergency's and unexpected bills. Things like; illnesses, car problems, traveling, unexpected pregnancy, a room-mate moving out, a pet bill, traffic tickets, car tags, insurance deductibles, or emergency home repairs?

Just one unexpected bill could set you back hundreds or thousands of dollars and put you in the hole with your regular monthly expenses. How would this affect your credit and ultimately your whole life! Much of your life revolves around your credit score, it's all intertwined. The bricks can be all lined up and then one brick pulled out of place and your whole world could crumble!

So why not *select* a "career" that pays more than just enough to get by. Start doing your research on career salaries. Consider every job, especially consider the most unusual jobs that no one ever hears about. Go to the library and research "Occupations of the USA." Get some ideas by asking people what was the most unusual occupation they ever heard of someone doing.

The strategy here is to find an occupation that's in demand and pays well, at least well over $35,000 per year. Of course you want an occupation that you are also comfortable with, or what's the point! But do the math . . . which would you rather have, an occupation that you don't like and it pay low wages or an occupation that you don't like and it pays very well. Or would you rather have a lower paying occupation with less responsibility, but one that you are happy with? That may suffice for a while, but, you may find yourself content at work but still frustrated with your constant accumulation of debt. A lot of people choose the "Happy at Work" with less responsibility with low wages and the financial debts eventually robs them of their Happiness.

There are plenty of higher paying jobs that you can be happy with. You have to do your own research. You also have to consider what kind of person you are. If you don't like public contact on a regular basis, then don't pick a career that puts you in that position.

Pick your career very carefully. Know your own strengths and weaknesses. Ask five different people to evaluate your personality; they may have a good idea of what kind of career you should have. Of course you have to make the ultimate decision. Money isn't everything . . . but having some left over at the end of the month sure beats being broke!

Sure, some people make over $65,000 a year and are still broke all the time. They are over extending themselves and need to make plenty of adjustments. But, if you make just enough to pay minimum living expenses, what adjustments can you make? You have zero options!

Economic disparity contributes greatly to a lack of education, poverty, drugs and certain crimes. Don't just think of yourself, think about the children you may have someday. Will you be able to help your children progress if you are barely surviving yourself?

Now, is the time to plan and set-up your life, don't wait.
Most of these occupations pay over $65,000 per year.

1. Accountant
2. Air Traffic Controller
3. College Professor
4. Computer Analyst
5. Curriculum Developer
6. Dietitian/Nutritionist
7. Environmental Scientist
8. Film Director/Movie
9. Financial Advisor
10. Heavy Equipment Operator
11. Human Resources Manager
12. Lab Technologist
13. Landscape Architect
14. Market Research Analyst
15. Massage Therapist
16. Medical Scientist
17. Meeting/Convention planner
18. Mental Health Counselor
19. Occupational Therapist
20. Paralegal
21. Pharmacist
22. Physical Therapist
23. Physician Assistant
24. Public Relations Specialist
25. Roughneck-Toolpusher-Drillers/Oil Rig Offshore
26. Real Estate Appraiser
27. Registered Nurse
28. Software Engineer
29. Technical Writer
30. Train Conductor
31. Veterinarian

Find more detailed information in the Occupational Outlook Handbook, from the Bureau of Labor Statistics (www.bls.gov)

What will your Business Card Say?

Junk e-mail & Spamming

You've got Mail, it should say; you've got "junk mail." Most would agree that 95% of e-mail is garbage. However, if you scan through some of it, you'll get tricked by a catch phrase in the subject line that sucks you in with some kind of scheme to get your money. Much of the internet is a game and full of people whose objective is to get money out of your pockets and into their hands!

When you sign up for a subscription or enter your name and address into anything, there is the possibility that you will be placed on some kind of junk mail list. You can avoid this by going on line and finding the "opt-out" e-mail web site. You can register to stop getting junk email. It won't stop all of it, but it will stop some of it.

Spamming is punishable now, get caught and you could face jail time.

Also be careful about those credit card offers sent through your email or slow mail. You can get off their mass list or pre-approved credit card offers by calling the opt-out phone line at:
1-888-5-OPTOUT (1-888-567-8688). Opt out- so you won't receive those annoying applications to sign up for pre-approved credit cards. Someone can steal your mail and order a credit card and ruin your credit before you even know it.

Languages

The younger you are the easier it is to learn a foreign language. You should consider learning a second language; it will definitely come in handy. Spanish seem to be the next biggest language in the USA after English. With more and more Hispanics relocating to the USA, you will most likely have use for it in the near future and even when traveling to other countries.

The USA has had a continuous growth in the Spanish population. Here are some headlines from internet searches: May 1, 2006 Protest by the Spanish community, May 1st to protest "The Great American Boycott 2006" and May 1, Day without Latinos.

The Census Bureau reported; "a surge in the Mexican population in the United States paced the explosive growth among Hispanics over the past decade, the Census Bureau reported, with newcomers settling in the Midwest as well as traditional immigrant gateways like Texas, California and Florida."

There are plenty of advantages in being bi-lingual and many job openings are now seeking people that speak both English and Spanish for various positions. The more languages you know, the more communication you will have with other groups of people. Lots of people admit that they wished they had learned a foreign language when they were younger. You never know what your future might bring. Also consider other languages such as: Chinese, Arabic, Dutch, and French.

Laziness or Fatigue

Some people use the term laziness too loosely. Of course there are some lazy people in the world. However in today's society there are a lot of energy deficient people. Take for instance a person who eats healthy and maintains a fit body. Now consider the junk food eater who never exercises. You can predict which one will most likely have the most energy. Is the junk-food-eater lazy or just tired?

Those with poor eating habits will *tire out* quicker than those who eat properly and exercise on a regular basis. Laziness is: the unwillingness to work or use your energy, and showing a lack of effort. If you don't have any energy, can you really be classified as being lazy. Probably more tired than lazy. A poor diet can make you physically and mentally lazy. So to avoid laziness due to fatigue, select a better diet. Choose more healthy foods, like fruits, nuts and vegetables. The body takes more energy to break down unhealthy foods than healthy foods. You can avoid that sluggish feeling you get from packing the body with unhealthy calories by eating a more natural diet. The more junk food you put into your body, the harder it has to work just to squeeze out nutrients and get rid of the toxins. Not drinking enough water can make you weak, yet, drinking too much water in a short amount of time can make you feel sluggish. Sipping water throughout the day is best.

So the next time someone calls you lazy . . . think about your diet. Are you mentally or physically tired from being over worked, or are you tired from lack of nutrition and eating junk food all week? (See: Nutrition)

Loneliness & Being Alone

Loneliness is not the same as being alone. You can be alone by yourself in your apartment and not be lonely. Loneliness is a state of mind, like an ill feeling of longing and yearning for someone to be with you to share your time. Every human on earth will experience loneliness at some time in their lives. Some will spend a great deal of time in a lonely state of mind because they don't have that special person in their life. Whatever the reason, there will be a certain amount of loneliness throughout our lives. Some people live with constant loneliness, some live with periodical loneliness. But most of the time we maintain what we feel we can bare. Then we look for ways to distract or get rid of our loneliness.

On the other hand there are several people in this world who prefer to be "alone," and they don't feel strange for being non-sociable. Many people go through phases of being anti-social. Usually this is for a select period of time and primarily by choice. Sometimes they are extremely particular about who they want to share their time with and sometimes staying focused on an objective without any social distractions may help a person stay optimistic about their future goals. This can last a few days or a few years depending on the person, and they "may" feel some loneliness during this time or maybe not.

Making Mistakes

In life, you are going to "Make Mistakes." However, if you can avoid making mistakes by having prior knowledge; are you willing to condition yourself to accept the knowledge of others? One example is; extending your education when you have the opportunity and the means to. What have you heard and seen in the majority of people who choose not to extend their education verses the ones who have? Ten years from now how is your decision going to affect you? Some things are pretty obvious, like "most" people without a degree will be stuck in low paying jobs, or jobs without advancement. A few become entrepreneurs, but most will live from paycheck to paycheck.

One way to avoid some mistakes in life is to do this exercise:

Take a good look at two people you know in your immediate environment; then think of two people you admire from afar (people that you don't know personally), maybe someone in an occupation that you are considering. Now, think about the mistakes the ones in your environment has made; whether they are now successful or not. Ask them about the two biggest mistakes they made in their life. Just see what they say.

Then do some research on the two people who you admire from afar. Locate a biography on them and examine it to see what mistakes they admit they have made in their lives. This will help you avoid making some of the same mistakes others have made, it will put you one step ahead in achieving your own goals in life.

Marriage

Most of us want to get married at sometime in our lives. Some of us dream of the marriage proposal, the wedding day, having children and living the story-book life.

Marriage is a good thing when two people are **compatible** with each other. This should mean; you love each other, you are good friends, you respect each other, you are considerate and honest with each other. You should also have "similar" ideas about; marriage, family, children, sex, money management, politics and religion. And if you can not find a balance in your relationship regarding these subjects . . . then you should NOT consider marriage. If you are too different from each other, it will be only a matter of time before you find that you cannot tolerate each others differences.

On the other hand, if you have discussed in detail each of the nine subjects below, and you have the same or similar ideas about each, you should be able to have a healthy relationship.
If you are thinking about marriage, consider the following:

Communication - How well do you and your mate communicate? Do you understand each other "most" of the time? Do you consider yourself friends as well as lovers?

Respect - Do you respect each other? How about when you are angry? What do you consider --crossing the line?

Consideration - Will you both clean-up the house, how about cooking? What about religion, voting, and racism; are you in strong disagreement on any of these issues?

Honesty - Are you willing to be honest with each other all of the time, or most of the time?

Marriage - What exactly does marriage mean to each of you? Are one of you "Conservative" and the other "Liberal?" Are either of you committed to different religious or moral beliefs? Is marriage counseling something you both would agree to in the future? Will you both wear your wedding rings?

Relatives - What roles will your relatives play in your marriage? Will either of you allow family members to interfere with your marriage. How often will they phone or visit?

Sex – How important is it for the both of you. What's acceptable and what is not?

Children - What kind of plans do you have for children? Will birth-control be solely one person's responsibility? What if one of you believe in spanking and the other does not?

Money Management - Who will be in charge of the money? Will you have separate accounts? Will it be negotiable for change in the future? Will you live on one income or do you agree that both of you will work all the time if possible?

Discuss these topics with your partner BEFORE saying "I Do." You can also send them an email to respond to if you feel it will be less awkward. If they think it's corny and don't want to discuss it, then you already have a communication problem to begin with. Think hard about it! Choosing the wrong mate can set you back socially, emotionally and financially . . . . So—don't ruin your life by letting your emotions control your common sense!
(See: Dating, Relationships)

Memories of Childhood

Some of us have good memories of childhood, but some of our memories of childhood aren't anything close to the likeness of a perfect childhood. Bad memories will aggravate you and frustrate you all through your young adult years. When you reflect on your childhood, you will remember the things you've seen, heard and felt, and how certain things appeared.

But you may not have the right facts; so have talks with your parents, read behavioral books, and talk with counselors. This way you will get a better understanding of what was going on throughout your childhood. Much of it you will be right about, but still, some of your facts may be inaccurate. Sometimes the picture is blatant and clear, but sometimes there is a different side of a situation that you may not have seen or heard. So try not to be hell-bent on harboring hostility for you parents without knowing all the facts. You may still be angry after you have heard all of the facts. If so, now you must begin to work through the pain and on to forgiveness. Why. . .

There is nothing healthy about feeling anger and contempt for anyone for a long period of time. And some things you must lighten your heart about in order to move to your next level of inner tranquility. If you were abused in your childhood, talk to someone about it. Talk to a counselor, confide in an older intelligent friend or join a self-improvement chat-line on the internet for moral support. Once you have gotten it out into the open, you can start healing and feeling better about yourself. You will find you are not alone, so many others have been raised in dysfunctional households too. More than you would guess. And the fortunate ones with untainted childhoods will find it hard to believe or even understand the pain and anger of someone who grew up in a dysfunctional family.

Once you start to forgive others, your self-esteem will improve and you will have a better emotional balance whenever you are angry or upset about something. You will start to understand the deeper reasons behind what angers you and why, which will help you to deal with the frustrations and complications that come with everyday life. You may not want to—but, get counseling now. If you are totally opposed to counseling, then buy two books on self- improvement and dealing with abuse or growing up in a dysfunctional household. Don't wait ten years from now when the deep-seated anger has ruined several personal relationships, your career, or even your life.

Everyone has some anger and resentment with their parents once they start thinking back to their childhood. Most people hold a "tiny bit" of resentment for what their parents did do, or didn't do; although some will never admit it. Just ask around, "most" people did not have a perfect **childhood** and your parents most likely didn't either! You were their first experiment, that is . . . they didn't have a set of children to practice raising before you came along. So, there were a lot of guess work going on while raising you.

When you get older and if you are a forgiving type of person, your opinion of your parents will change some. Especially once you have your own children. The picture will be clearer and you will understand a lot more about life. Blame never fixed anything! And, you will make "different mistakes" in raising your own children. But some of you have great parents and you look to them always for support in all your decision making. This is good and you are the fortunate.

Always try to focus mostly on the "happy times" you shared with your family. Don't hold grudges forever, it only damages your mental and physical health in along run.

Military Service

The Military can be an alternative to going to College. It can offer you a career in over 120 occupations along with on the job training and some programs to help with college after you complete your enlisted term of duty. Check with a recruiter or go on-line for a list of military occupations available. Unlike the private sector, in the military you can retire with a pension after 20 years of active duty service. Most private corporations required you to be employed for 30 years before you can retire with a pension.

The main branches of the military services are:

United States Air Force
United State Marine Corps
United States Army
United States Navy
United States Coast Guard

The National Guard is a component of the United States Army. The Navy and the Marines work closely with one another on several military bases. The Marines are usually the first to go into battle. The U.S. Coast Guard protects the water and costal lines for the United States.

Each branch of service is divided into "Commissioned Officers" and enlisted personnel who are also referred to as; "Non-Commissioned Officers." Commissioned Officers are

are mostly recognized in "dress" uniform by having their rank worn on their lapels or collars with such emblems as: stars, leafs, or gold or silver bars; and are required to have some previous College.

Once you sign-up for one of the five military branches, you are required to serve between two and four years of "active duty" service and two or more years of "inactive" reserve service. That depends on the branch of service and its contract. You can sometimes select which occupational field you would like to get trained in.

If you are injured while in the military, you qualify for disability. Once enlisted, you automatically have life insurance. If you die or are accidentally killed, your beneficiary will get a designated amount.

Once you have completed your active duty in service and have gotten an "Honorable Discharge" you may be selected for a civilian job quicker than a high school graduate or other applicants, simply because you are a Veteran with O.J.T. (on the job training).

The Marines, the Army and the Special Forces are by far the most rugged of the military forces.

Modeling

Everyone isn't meant to become a fashion model, so, if this is not your dream then don't let anyone pressure you into becoming a model. However, if you are interested, be cautious; because you are young, you have a "particular" beauty and people will be attracted to you for various reasons.

No matter if you are interested or not, you may be approached by someone claiming to be a talent or modeling recruiter. First, they will tell you how beautiful you are and then offer you a business card and ask you to come by for a fashion shoot. Never go anywhere with a stranger. If you have never heard of their company before, see if you can find the agency on-line or in the telephone directory. Call and ask questions about the agency. Ask questions about how much their photo sessions costs and how much modeling classes costs. Find out what kind of percentage you will get if you are hired as a model. Find out which companies they have supplied models for and how often?

A lot of these agencies will take your money for Modeling classes and will never help you find modeling work after you have completed the classes. Do the math, most of these companies will take your money and give you little in return except a temporary pumped-up ego and a few glamorous pictures of yourself.

Remember, if a modeling agency really sees potential in you, they will offer to do a photo shoot of you for free, simply because they know that you will be in demand and most likely will bring them a profit. They get paid a percentage of your earnings if you are hired out on a job.
It's a good idea to talk to someone in the Modeling business; research modeling magazines and newsletters on line.

Beware of photo shoots especially someone who wants to take pictures of you at their private home or private studio.

Always take a friend with you and let others know where you will be and what time you are expected to be back. Never sign any contracts that you are not sure of. If someone will not let you take the contract with you to review at home, then it's probably not a good idea to sign it on the spot. Make sure the contract has an expiration date preferably six months to two years. And be extra careful in taking pictures that will be used for "internet use" or having "electronic rights." Never sign anything that you are not sure of. Just say "*you are not comfortable with signing that right now*" and ask to take a copy of the contract with you. Let an intelligent older person or an attorney review it. **Never take nude pictures, and never let anyone convince you to let them take nude pictures of you.** Snap-shots or motion pictures will come back to haunt you in the future! Once an image has entered the eye of the camera, you can never take it back. Never take nude photos for money and never do it with someone you are dating, it almost always has a negative consequence in the end.

Never be so narcissistic, vain, or conceited that you are willing to go to someone's house on the spur of the moment because they have told you how beautiful or photogenic they think you are. Whether you are male of female, don't let them tempt you to go to their place to do a small photo "test shoot" for them. Most likely they are praying upon your innocence and want personal favors from you. It could be dangerous.

If ever in your modeling pursuits things don't feel right, go with you intuition. If you are suspicious of something—just don't do it. Tell them you will get back with them tomorrow and find a "calm convincing" way out of the bad situation. You suddenly feel ill, or you just realized you were supposed to meet someone are good excuses. If you are having any serious doubt whether you should participate in something; consider it your intuition telling you . . . NOT to!

Sex slavery trafficking is on the rise;
Predators get teenagers involved in prostitution by tricking them into meeting them someplace. They will then drug you and take you someplace remote and keep you locked in a room in a secluded area. Pimps will sometimes take you to a different state or foreign country and force you to have sex with strangers and then sell you to other pimps after a few months. Meanwhile they are keeping you drugged and keeping your money to prevent you from getting help.

(See: Sex Predators)

Motivation

Self-Motivation is the primary reason successful people are successful. You are primarily responsible for your own motivation. Sometime others can help motivate you, but, "you" have to have an unquenchable thirst to want to obtain your chosen goal(s). It simply has to be inside of "you."

To continuously set goals without the enthusiasm to accomplish them is pointless. If you <u>do not</u> have a strong enough "reason" to set your mind on a particular goal, then you won't have the motivation to accomplish it.

You can build motivation and inspiration through reading books, watching movies, group discussions or examining the accomplishments of other people. You may even want to make a collage of pictures and post them on a wall in you home to remind you to be diligent in reaching your goals. Staying "focused" in-it-self will give you a certain amount of self-motivation. Always stay enthusiastic about life, even though it will deal you more than a few blows. Don't let the downs push you into despair. Life is about "topping the mountains" and "hitting the valleys" with grace; it's constantly changing. Accepting change will help you to accept the many winds of life. Think of a "reason" that will give you enough motivation to accomplish "one" goal you have set. Write it down.

Motivation is a psychological enthusiasm that is manifested within you!

Music

Lyrical music is somewhat of a programming device. It programs the mind. The old folks will tell you, garbage in . . . garbage out! We are constantly programmed from the moment of birth. We are first influenced by our parents. But when we reach those young adult years we want to rebel against most of what we were taught. But if you think about it . . . your parents pretty much gotten you where you are so far —which isn't all bad.

We learn by repetition. We learn by repetition, we learn by repetition. We learned our ABC's by saying them over and over. The music you listen to programs your mind and subsequently your actions. So be careful of the lyrics you allow to float into your ears. Ask yourself, would you want "YOUR" younger sibling or own children listening to certain songs? You have the answer within yourself why you should be selective in what kinds of music you let enter into your ears. You have a choice. Remove negative music from your ears, it only brings out the worst in you. Just like being around negative people on a regular basis, you will eventually start picking up some of their negative ways. Any anger or hostility or contempt you have in life only worsens with negative music and it can only help you down the wrong road.

Condition yourself for your future. Remember that horror movie that you didn't want to see because the vision stays locked in your mind for days. What you "see" and "hear" stays in your conscious for a long time.
When you are a young adult, music helps program your character. What are you programming yourself for?

Negative People

Just like negative music . . . Negative people are just as bad. Stop surrounding yourself with *Negative* friends and associates. Negative people are just like "Bad Food" they poison the brain and drain your positive energy. For simplicity sake, let's just say there are basically two kinds of energy forces in people; the "negative" kind and the "positive" kind. How to recognize them . . . ?

Negative people drain your energy and motivation to achieve anything in life. They will ignore your ideas and your accomplishments. They will not help drive your motivation and they will always give you a reason why you won't be able to accomplish your goals. They will always throw monkey-wrenches in your ideas and tell you how you can't do whatever it is you are striving to accomplish; and they will not give you a valid reason why your ideas or plans won't work. Negative people love to see you frustrated and off-balance, this is just part of their character.

Positive people are energy givers. After a conversation with them you will most likely FEEL optimistic and cheerful. Your spirit will be up and you will be full of energy for the next few days. Although positive people may question your intentions, they will not do so in an antagonizing way. They mostly want to offer helpful advice. Positive people want to lend a hand because they are concerned about your future; therefore they will try to help prevent you from making any huge mistakes.

After having a conversation with someone, always think about what was said and whether it was in your best interest. Always consider the "message" that they were trying to communicate to you.

Nutrition

Just LOOK around you, the world is full of people who are poorly nourished; fast food junkies, smokers, excessive drinkers, etc. Poor nutrition means that your body is not getting adequate enzymes to feed good cells. Your body must replace dead cells and kill off the free-radicals that enter the body through contamination found in the air, food, and water. Poor nutrition will cause your body to eventually mal-function in some area or another and create its own internal enemies such as cancer.

For instance, an alcoholic's kidneys, liver, or heart will fail or become diseased because the body is getting an over-load of toxic fluid. The kidneys can't flush out the toxins as fast as the Alcoholic puts it in. So over time, the body's organs will become faulty and eventually shut down. Kind of like a performance engine, if you repeatedly fill it with bad gas that is below specification grade and don't change the oil and filters as required, the engines valves and parts become clogged and can't produce the energy and combustion that it once had. So the engine fails to operate at full capacity. The same goes for the body; good nutrition is gas for your body. A proper diet is essential if you want to stay healthy.

You can maintain a healthy body if you:

1. Limit the use of; prescription and over-the-counter drugs.
2. Minimize or eliminate alcoholic beverages.
3. Eat less processed foods; processed foods are foods that are altered from their natural state, such as packaged and labeled foods.
4. Eat organic foods. Organic foods are foods that are grown "without" chemical fertilizers.

5. Take balanced multi-vitamin supplements and herbs daily.
6. Cleanse your colon on a regular basis; once or twice a month.

……………………………………………………

Buy a book on herbs and vitamins; study them to get a better understanding of how the body works. Research the causes of diseases and deficiencies in the body. This knowledge can help you live a longer healthier life.

Remember: What you do to your body while you are "young" will play a huge role in what diseases you may have to deal with when you are "older." So try to at least be good to your body in the first thirty years.

Fruit, Nuts, and **Vegetables;**

are necessary because they are the fiber and bulk that help push the toxins out of your body. With out them, feces can hang around in your intestines for days, making you feel sluggish and weak.

Note: Always wash fruits and vegetables thoroughly before eating; they often carry bacteria or parasites on them.

Older Acquaintance

Most of the older people in your life will want the best for you and will try to help you achieve your goals. However, after you leave home you may run into that older person who sees you as prey. It's not so easy to be a good judge of character especially when you have not yet experienced various situations in life. There are two kinds of older acquaintances, the ones who try to help you and make life a little simpler for you. And the ones who have hidden motives and their objective is to miss-use you.

If you are not sure about the motives of an older person, question them why they are offering to help you and ask them if you are going to "owe" them anything for their help. Always know what you are getting yourself into. If they seem irritated because you are questioning them . . . they are probably up to no good. A "kind" person "gives" from the goodness of their heart and a "devious" person "gives" to see what they can get in return. Never let an older person take advantage of you in any way! Never lie, steal, or cheat for them or exchange sexual favors for them. Be mindful to never *position* yourself to be taken advantage of. And if you have been taken advantage of in the past by an older person, talk to an adult who you can trust about it, they can help you make the right decision.

But remember, an adult who gives you everything you "want" but not necessarily "need" is not helping you grow up and develop into a mature and responsible person. They are teaching you to be "dependant" not "independent."

(See: Caution)

Parties

Of course we all like to party while we are young—being in a relaxed atmosphere with our own peers and not having our parents around to tell us what we cannot do is very attractive. Most young adults find it hard to resist this enticing environment. However, parties can sometimes turn out to be disastrous if too many rules are broken! Drinking and driving can lead to destruction of property. Drugs can lead to unprotected sex or rape. Sometimes fights breakout over something petty and lead to death.

First of all, you should never go to a party alone, always take a friend. You should never go to a party if you heard roomers of gangs planning of being there. Never go to a party where there will be a storm of disagreements. Now-a-days you don't know who's caring a knife or a gun. You know by now that young adults are more likely to settle a disagreement with a weapon than a fist fight like the old days. So look out for yourself, use your "intuition" and if you feel something is about to *start,* find a safe place or leave the party area. You wouldn't want to be paralyzed for the rest of your life over a heated argument turned violent.

Never go to a party to start a fight, and if someone is drunk or high, do not provoke them. They are not in their right mind. Let it go! No need to wind up dead or in jail over something that could have been avoided.

Remember to stay away from
"Wrong Crowds"
you know the ones that have a "high potential" for acquiring felonies.

Don't be a drifter!
Stay Focused on your Goals!

Spend too much of your youth
hanging out— doing nothing; you will most likely regret it before your twenty-ninth birthday.

PETS

If you choose to own a pet, consider the following:

- Will your lifestyle allow you to give your pet the attention it needs on daily basis?
- Do you live in a pet friendly environment?
- Can you afford to take your pet to the Veterinarian if it gets hurt or sick?
- What if your pet bites someone, can you assume responsibility such as court costs?
- Can you afford to feed them a proper diet and feed yourself too?
- Can you afford a trainer, or do you think yelling and abusing your pet is ok?
- Are you patient enough to give *proper* love and appreciation for a pet?
- Does your roommate approve, or are they allergic to certain animals?
- Will a confined pet be happy within his or her environment?
- Can you afford to get your pet spayed or neutered?
- Can you afford regular vaccinations for your pet?
- Who's going to baby-sit your pet when you leave town?
- How will you handle the death of a pet or the decision to put them to sleep?

Owning a pet is a lot of responsibility and can almost seem like taking care of an infant. They will need to be cared for patiently and "continuously." You can't pack them up and ship them to Alaska when you get tired of them. You will have to clean-up after them and feed them on a daily basis. A lot of people like the glamorous side of owning a pet but fail to realize the huge responsibility of actually taking care of one. Always look before you leap. Ask someone that has a pet what it is like. Also, try baby-sitting a friends pet for a few days to get a real feel of what owning a pet is like. Pets are easy to get . . . but not so easy to give away or get rid of. So make sure you have thought it out step-by-step before taking on this huge responsibility!

PICTURES

Every year appreciate who you are and how you have changed. Take pictures of yourself! Don't feel that you are being vain and don't worry that others will think you are conceited. Later in life you will be happy that you took pictures while you were young. Also, your children will want to know what you looked like when you were their age.

Some of us don't like to take pictures, while others are always hamming it up for the cameras. Cameras and camcorders, use them as much as possible. It's good to keep memories of how you looked years ago. Take pictures of your family and friends too. Ask older people if they have a lot of pictures of themselves when they were younger. Most will say that they don't have many pictures but wished they had. Send copies or negatives to family or friends for safe keeping. In your young adult life you will probably move around a few times before settling down to one location. Take pictures every year and be sure to put the date and locations on them.

Bring a camera or camcorder to those special events. Also take pictures on common days too, that's part of your life. Have fun, Smile for the Camera . . .

There's Nothing like a moment "Captured" in Time!

(See: Modeling)

Pranks

Playing a small prank on someone is pretty funny as long as no one gets hurt, *and* both parties can laugh about it latter. Some T.V. shows like "Punked" show pretty harmless pranks because they are well thought out and they don't destroy the integrity of a person or do them any permanent harm.

But, if at the end of the prank, only one side is laughing, then the prank was most likely in bad taste. You should never pull pranks on people you don't like, it will only be received as a disguise to do them some kind of harm and you could get into a lot of trouble for it.

Never pull a prank that has the potential of going wrong or being deadly, you could wind up paying a lot of fines or even going to jail. Think long and hard before engaging in this sort of self-amusement.

Be careful about practical jokes,
they may not leave you laughing!

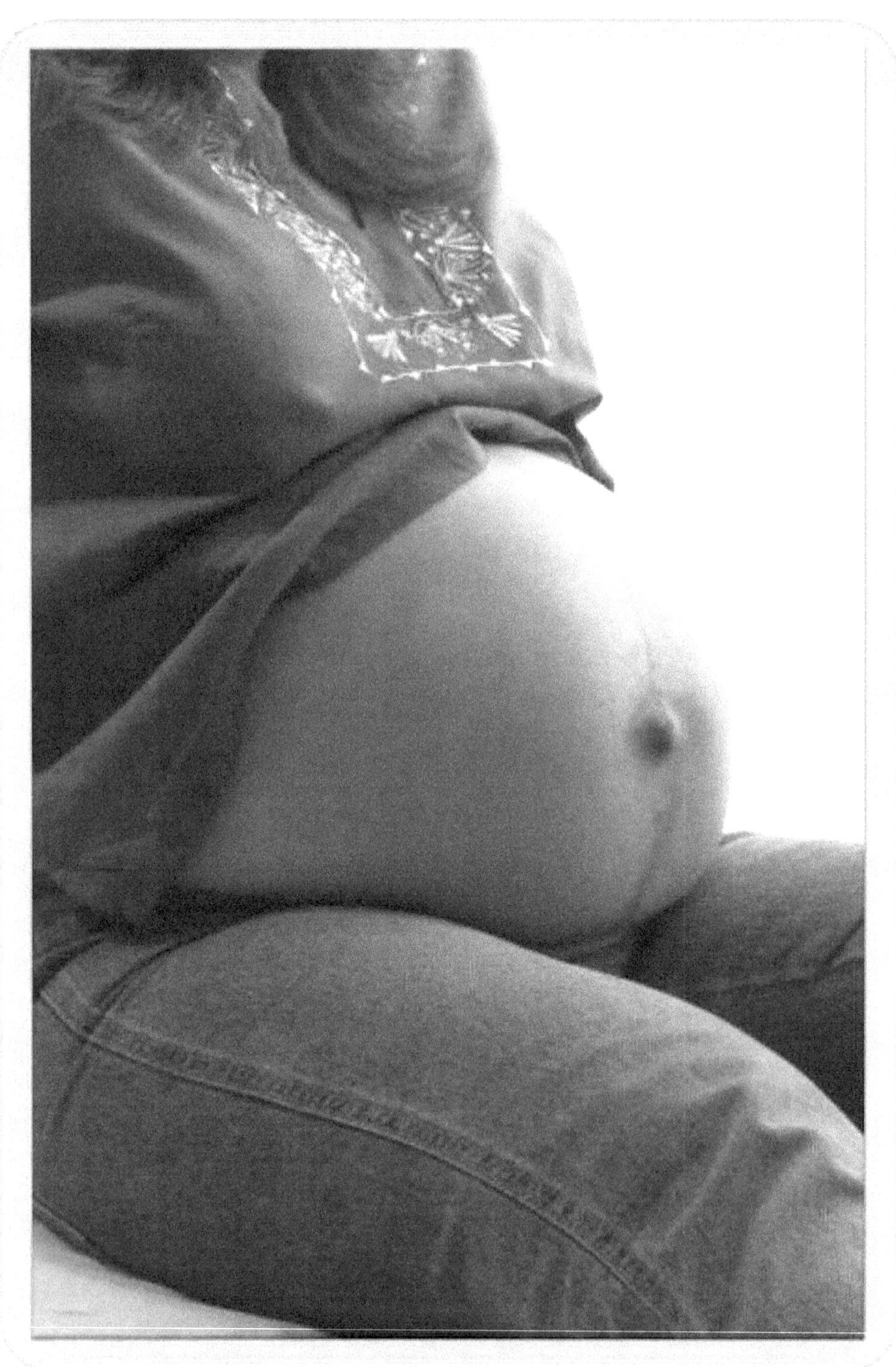

Pregnancy

You already know that abstinence is the best protection against pregnancy. But, if you find that you cannot control yourself because your "hormones" are the problem and "they" are forcing you to have sex . . . then do the logical thing, use protection! Use a condom and a sperm killing cream, and ladies remember to use your doctor prescribed contraception.

They are still working on a new contraception method for men. You should never have sex just to impress or entrap your partner; in the end, it won't work out the way you had planned. Consider the innocent child!

Gentlemen, you are "ALSO" responsible for unplanned pregnancies. Better wrap it up! Birth control does <u>not</u> work after the fact. You must use it before the intercourse starts. Always have your protection available ahead of time. Be prepared. Carry condoms in your purse or wallet, you might even help save a friend from an unplanned pregnancy.

Don't be a statistic of teen pregnancy.

Nearly 40 percent of American women become pregnant before their twentieth birthday and most teen pregnancies are unplanned.

If you do become pregnant and need financial help, then apply for Medicaid; you should see a doctor right away. If you do not want to go to a conventional doctor . . . then see a "Legitimate" Holistic Herbal Doctor. You have a choice. But you will need to eat right and take some kind of pre-natal vitamins to make sure your child is properly nourished. Certain vitamin deficiencies in pregnant women can lead to all kinds of child deformities and disorders.

Remember; everything you swallow, breathe, or smoke flows through your unborn child's veins. And a sickly child is a whole lot harder to raise than a healthy one.

Processed Food

"Processed Foods" are foods which have been "altered" from its naturally grown out-of-the-ground state. Such as: pre-cooked frozen meals, food cooked and canned, boxed and packaged snacks, cereal, pastas, bread and jelly; and condiments such as ketchup, mustard and relish. Pretty much any food that is packaged and comes with a label listing the *added* ingredients and *calories* are all processed foods. Processed foods will most likely contain preservatives in order to extend the shelf life of the food.

In this era it's hard to live without some processed foods because we are conditioned by the processing plants. They use several groups of people as "food testers" to help them find the most favorable flavors so they can easily market them to their consumers (us) via the grocery stores.

"Un-processed Foods" or "Natural Foods"are usually found in the "Produce Department," which is the fruit and vegetables section of the grocery store. They are foods such as: Apples, oranges, bananas, grapes, avocados, broccoli, onions, potatoes, carrots, tomatoes and raw nuts.

Although food preservatives such as: sulfur dioxide, potassium-sorbate, benzoic acid and sodium nitrite are all necessary in helping processed foods stay fresh, they sometimes interfere with the body's natural chemical balance. Also, many fruit drinks, carbonated drinks, candy, and chewing gum contain hidden chemicals such as: Aspartame also named Equal or (NutraSweet), Saccharin also named Sweet 'N Low or Sugar Twin, and Sucralose who's product name is Splenda. Using sugar substitutes instead of sugar can lower your risk of tooth decay, but just like preservatives they may not agree with your body. And some groups will argue that there are thousands of synthetic chemicals allowed to be used in foods when they believe that some have been known to cause cancer.

Nearly all "Fast Food" chains and some restaurants use processed foods to cook with. With each "process" the nutritional value of the food is diminished and it <u>loses</u> nourishment. Which means the food is broken down and many necessary vitamins and minerals are lost. Therefore you will need to eat "more food" to get the same amount of energy to run your body. Overeating causes you to gain excessive weight and makes your body more receptive to diseases by keeping your immune system from operating at its best.

<u>Helpful tips:</u>

Instead of eating potato chips, eat some raw nuts, instead of a slice of cake; eat a pear, apple or some grapes. Instead of pancakes and bacon, eat some bananas and oranges. Always incorporate some green leafy vegetables in your daily diet; chop parsley and greens, mix with an egg, season and fry like a pancake. Try to set good eating habits now while you are young, and try not to acquire a taste for mostly processed foods. By eating natural foods on a regular basis, you are also **conditioning** your taste buds to like healthy foods instead of processed foods.

Procrastination

Procrastination kills Aspiration! The longer you put off accomplishing something, the less desire you'll have to do it. The old saying "don't put-off for tomorrow what you can do today" is a rule that successful people live by. If you continue to push aside your desires in life, they become fuzzy and will eventually disappear. When you are young you are full of desires, and if you don't make the necessary effort to achieve them, you will regret it later on in life. So if you don't want to be old and dreaming about the chance you had to realize your dreams, stop procrastinating and create some kind of practical plan. Positive thoughts must precede continuous action towards your goals.

Don't procrastinate, it will become perpetual if you do. Do your chores on time, do your studying on time and never let things pile up. It makes the task much harder to complete tomorrow. Leave procrastination for those who have nothing to achieve in life.

A Little Story about Procrastination

There was once a young boy who wanted to become an actor. And when he was a senior in high school he took-up acting classes for the whole year. Then he started college that following year. He said he would work on his acting career just as soon as he finishes college. Then when he graduated from college, he went on vacation a met a beautiful woman. Then he said he will work on his acting career right after he got married. And when he got married he said he would work on it before his first child was born. And after his first born was born, he said he would work on his acting career before the second child was born. And when the second child was born he said he will work on his acting career before he turned thirty. And on his thirtieth birthday, he said that he would work on his acting career just as soon as he saved up ten thousand dollars. And when he had saved up ten thousand dollars, he said he would start his acting career after he bought his first home. And after he bought his first home, he said that he would pursue his acting career before his children went to high school. And when they both started high school he said he would work on his acting career before they graduated. And at his sons graduation from high school he said to him . . . son, never put off pursuing your dreams in life-- you may never get a second chance once the ball starts rolling!

Avoid being a "big time procrastinator" by not becoming a "small time procrastinator."

Write a note to yourself each night before you go to sleep of what you plan to do for the following day or week. Maybe you will need to shorten a telephone conversation, leave a party early or skip that dinner invitation-what ever it takes, just don't make excuses for not completing each task. Check them off as you complete them. You will feel good about yourself the next day after you finish a task.

(See: Motivation)

Race . . .
Being **Different!**

You didn't have a choice regarding your race. There are no blank squares to check-off in the womb to select what race you want to be. No matter what race we are all born for a reason! People will try to judge you by the color of your skin . . . by the shape of your eyes . . . by the type of hair on your head or the accent in your voice.

There are hundreds of hate groups in the world, and dozens of stereotypes for all races and nations of people. Everyone wants to be the "superior group." However, we must all strive to get along and appreciate all of our differences. If we were all the same we would still have complaints about each other. And still there would be "groups" who would try to make divisions because of eye color, hair color, height or weight. Man will always try to find a way to make himself feel superior to other mankind in some fashion.

God has given this world every human being that abides here, and we as humans don't have the power to create one single living organism from scratch. So why should we hate—what we cannot create?

Within every race, there is "good" and "bad."

Reading

Read something everyday! Read . . . Read . . . Read.

Every since you were young, you were always told to read. Why is it so important? Because "Knowledge is Power," the more you know, the greater your potential to acquire power. People with power are the ones who are in control, without knowledge you are at their mercy; especially regarding laws or social injustice. You may not like learning about history, but if you can comprehend exactly how it relates to the world you live in today, it will all make sense. Try to understand the development and the basic principles of the world. Such as the significance of the stock market and commodities market, the oil trades, the textile markets and the nations politics. Study the daily fluctuation of the money markets in foreign countries. Study how the United States is viewed by other countries and which countries are our allies and which are our enemies. These are things you should know just to understand how the world flows together. Not for any school grade, but for your own understanding of how countries connect with one another. The more you learn the more creative and innovative you'll become, which subsequently could lead to a more satisfying career opportunity or even entrepreneurial developments. Studies show that most people use less that 60% of their brains mental capacity . . . so, with all that hard drive available, why not use it.

Of course never believe "everything" that you read, take the part that makes the most sense and leave the rest behind. Remember, in some areas of life it's ok to think outside the box and not follow along with how everyone else is thinking.

Visit a book store or library every three months and find the subjects that interest you. Try to stick to one or two subjects until you have grasped the most important elements. A few good sections to start with are: "How To," "Self Improvement," "World History/Economics," and "Spiritual Awareness." The more you read, the more life makes sense.

Can't learn much from playing video games . . .
So pick up some books or magazines and read something!

Oh . . . You hate reading?
Then watch:

The History Channel . . .
The Discovery Channel . . .
The Biography Channel . . .
The Science Channel . . .
The Animal Channel . . .
The First 48 Hrs on the A & E Channel
FSTV (Free Speech T.V.)
LINK T.V.
Rent a "Documentary" from the Video Store or Library

Scan the radio or internet for interesting local or syndicated "Talk Radio Stations" You can also tune in and hear them on your computer speakers.

Quote-

> *"The recipe for perpetual ignorance is: be satisfied with your opinions and content with your knowledge."*
>
> *Elbert Hubbard*
> *U.S. Author (1856 - 1915)*

Relationships

One of the hardest things for a young adult in a relationship to do is, distinguish between being in love, or being in lust. Relationships are based on a lot more than just the physical. So never get involved in a relationship "only" because of physical attraction. Look past the physical to find out what you really have in common. When you are young, it's hard to really know who "You" are, which makes it especially hard to decide on what you "need" and "want" in a relationship.

Here are a few rules to consider when selecting a partner.

- Try to find someone who is compatible with you. Someone who shares the same interests, beliefs and values that you do. See how well you get along without T.V. or sex. See if you have a lot to talk about, or is there a huge effort to make conversation? Do you have outside activities you enjoy together, or is the air stale without T.V. or sexual activity?

- Make a list of the top seven things that are really important to you. See if your potential mate matches at least five of them. Opposites attract but your differences may not hold you together for very long.

- Ask yourself honestly if you really care about this person or are they there just to keep you from being lonely.

Remember any relationship should have; Honesty, Communication, Consideration and Respect. And if just "one" of these are missing, eventually, you find that you have wasted a lot of precious time. *A balance of "Compatibility," that's the Secret!*

(See: Dating, Internet Dating, Marriage)

Renting & Roommates

The first thing Young Adults want to do when they move away from home is . . . get their own apartment. But, chances are you can't afford to live alone in your own apartment. So you start to think about who you would like as a roommate. But remember the following:

Renting

You should never rent an apartment that is so expensive that you can not afford to pay the rent by your self for a couple of months if you need to. Your roommate may move out in the middle of the night two days before rent is due. Even if you both are on the lease and you plan to sue them for their portion of the rent, it could take several months. You might want to have enough saved up just in case something like this happens. It could take awhile before you find another roommate.

If you don't have a reliable vehicle, you should never rent an apartment that is not on a bus line; you may have to take the bus until your vehicle is repaired. You should try to find an apartment that has a short lease, just in case you need to move for some reason, you might change jobs or change schools. Also, you should spend several hours in the vicinity of the neighborhood you are thinking about living in. You should know what the area is like during the day and night before you relocate there.

Roommates

Remember, if you decide to make a current friend a roommate, most likely you will weaken the friendship or lose this person as a friend. Somehow making a good friend a roommate "kills" the friendship! Living with a friend and seeing all the irritating and aggravating things they do can change your opinion of them. Whether it's their super clean or super sloppy ways, you will discover the huge differences that you did not see in each other before you were roommates. So if you're going to get a roommate, you probably should not room-up with your very best friend. Instead find an associate that you feel you can reasonably get along with. Then, agree on some ground rules (in writing) that each of you want to live by.

As a young adult it's probably safer to have a roommate. However, when choosing a roommate, consider how they grew up and whether safety is a concern to them. Is locking the door, checking the peep-hole before opening the door, being very selective about who they invite over etc. important to them? What about relatives or local friends spending the night? What about groceries and cooking. What about quiet time in the apartment? Find out FIRST if you agree or disagree on certain dwelling matters.

Role Models

Some of the most successful people in this world had certain role models that they looked up to, studied, and pattern themselves after. It could be your own parents that set the foundation for your desire to accomplish and achieve. Some say that their mothers or fathers were their first role models. But others must go out side of the family to find people that inspire them enough to want to pattern themselves after. Some people feel that they are pioneers and that they don't need a role model. But most of us pull our energy to achieve and to be successful from someone we admire. Picking the right role model can help you to stay focused and on track in your younger years in life.

However, when choosing a role model you should know as much as possible about the person, both public and some private information about them before choosing to pattern yourself after them. Investigate their background; things like, their childhood, their parents, what schools they attended, what achievements they receive, the environment they grew up in, and what mistakes they made along the way; so you can avoid making the same ones.

When you get older, your desire for a role model will be less significant because you would have reached a certain plateau in your life that you are content with. No matter who you choose to model yourself after whether it is a Parent, Teacher, Politician, Scientist, Doctor, Actor, Musician or Artists; the benefits of selecting a "Positive" role model can greatly enhance your direction in life.

Safety at Night

When you move to your own apartment, you want to take serious precautions for insuring your safety at home as well as when you are out shopping, going to the movies, or out at the nightclub. No one wants to feel paranoid all day long and worried that someone is out to get them. But, as a young adult male or female you must take a certain amount of precaution to protect yourself from being prayed upon.

You should have a safety routine that you use on a daily basis, and maybe an alternate one that you can use when you go out to party. You must think about your "plan for safety" ahead of time, before you are in a confrontational situation. Have a plan that is most likely to work for you.

When leaving your home, remember that- the biggest indication of "no one is home" is . . . a dark and quiet house. Leaving a T.V. or radio on and using light timers can also mimic someone's at home. Remember, having a loud conversation on your cell phone when leaving or returning home puts you off guard. It also alerts predators and allows them to make observation of your schedule.

No one wants their home to be broken into and their stuff stolen when they are gone. But your biggest safety concern should be when "you are at home." If you cannot afford a monitored alarm system, you can buy an inexpensive version that has motion sensors for monitoring one or two rooms. Depending on how hard you sleep and the floor plan of your home, sleeping with your bedroom door closed and locked may not be a bad idea.

If your bedroom door is open-the intruder has freedom to enter any room without making any additional noise. You would probably want to prepare to protect yourself from the intruder before you wake up and find them standing at the foot of your bed.

However if you are a very light sleeper you might want to sleep with the door open; something to think about. Also having a telephone in the bathroom may not be a bad idea either.

- What is your plan if someone tries to follow you inside your apartment?
- What is your plan if someone breaks in while you are asleep?
- What is your plan if someone tries to assault you while entering or leaving your vehicle?
- Do you think that "first floor" apartments are safer?

Mace, stun guns and personal alarms are devices that can possibly protect you. You should know what the laws are for your particular state regarding stun guns, tasers and handguns. Never consider owing a handgun without learning to properly use it at a firing range. But remember, all weapons especially firearms "can be used against you" and there is always the possibility of someone innocent getting shot. Bullets do travel through walls and ceilings. If you own a dangerous device, always take safety precautions when children visit or live in your home.

Always call someone and let them know where you are going. Never go anywhere and not let someone know where you are going. Call someone, or at least leave a message on your own phone message box. Never go to sleep with open windows on the first or second floors and always lock your windows when you leave home. An unlocked window is an open invitation for burglars. Always make sure doors and window locks are secure.

Remember:
Regardless of the intentions, good or bad, when you are out in public, someone's eyes are on you . . . someone is always watching you.

Saving Money

"Saving Money" is by far one of the hardest things to do in life. Most people young or old have a hard time saving money. In order to set yourself apart from the "most people" crowd and include yourself in that small percentage that learned how to save a portion of their income on a "regular" basis; here's what you have to do.

> You have to *make a pact with yourself* and enforce it no matter what. If you plan to put one-fifth of your income away, you will need to set up a "fail safe" method of sticking-to-it. When you cash your check every two weeks or so, always have your deposit slip with you so you can make your regular deposit right into your savings account (if it's the same bank). Calculate how much money you will have if you saved just $200.00 a month. How much will you have in five years? Set yourself a long range plan. Maybe a down payment on a house or a newer car or a business investment might be your goal. Try to save and "pretend" that this money does not exist and try not to use it for anything until the end of your plan. Even if you changed plans as far as what you first wanted to use it for.

At least you will have a decent lump of cash saved up to do something with. In most cases, a house is a better investment than a vehicle. Vehicles depreciate rapidly, whereas houses "appreciate" in value. Meanwhile, don't over-extend yourself. Be especially careful in obtaining credit cards, they will most likely ruin your credit as they have for millions of people. Most people overspend especially on things they can't afford. You should not be spending half of your income on rent; instead your rent or mortgage should never be more than one-third of your monthly net-income. Learning to save money is easy for some and harder for others. It takes discipline and determination. Consider using a lay-a-way plan when shopping for clothes and furniture, that way if you realized that you went over your budget or get hit with some unexpected bill; you can choose to cancel your lay-a-way. Saving is so hard in this day and age because we as humans want to acquire things NOW, the faster the better, no one wants to wait and save for years for something they want next week. However, if you can manage to change your mind set and allow the patient side of your human nature to develop, you will definitely be ahead of the rest in the long run.

A lot of people have savings accounts but usually have less than $500.00 in them. One way to close the revolving door on your savings account is by using a checking account to pay your bills and never request a check card for your savings account, and if the bank sends you one, cut it up immediately! Also, never transfer money from your savings to your checking account. Remember, the only transactions that should be made on your savings account for the first five years are "Deposits Only!"

Read and research different kinds of "Investments," you may find some options for increasing your wealth.

(See: Holidays)

Scams

The world is full of all kinds of people who spend most of their lives gettin' over on other people, and sooner or later a few of their con tricks will cross your path.

There are all kinds of scams from: work-at-home, real estate investing, internet affiliate marketing, selling by classified ads, stock market investing, phishing and chain letters. Scammers will always entice you with fantastic stories about how much money you can make if you invest in their hair brained "fast money" making idea' when actually, they are the "only" ones who will be making any money. So you may as well keep your money in your pocket. Making a lot of money with little effort is always intriguing, but use your common sense. As they old saying goes . . . "If it sounds too good to be true . . . , it probably is too good to be True."

"Most" work at home job opportunity offers are scammers who charge a "small fee" for sending you information. They know—if they charged "large fees" they would have a lot of people after them. The scamming continues because, once someone realizes they have been "scammed" they most likely will not pursue the scammer. Some scammers try to convince you to be unethical too, by having you repeat their stupid making money process. But if you make your money by tricking and deceiving others, it may one day come back to haunt you and some scammers have even been prosecuted for fraud.

Don't waste your money and don't fall pray to any of these common work-at-home, or home-based business opportunities scams.

1. Medical Billing or Typing At Home
2. Chain letters or Pyramid Schemes
3. Envelop Stuffing or Craft Assembly
4. E-mail Processing
5. (some) Multi-Level Marketing (MLM)

-Phishing, is when someone sends fraudulent email pretending to be from a legitimate company like, your "insurance company," your "bank," or "your "internet provider" asking you to provide confidential information. If you give them the requested information they can use it to commit identity theft and tap into your accounts or sell your information to someone else. Never send personal information over the internet in response to an e-mail. Many scammers will mimic legitimate companies. Always contact the company by telephone by using a legitimate phone number that you "already" have for them, or contact them by postal mail using an address that you already have in your file.

If you want to know the "tricks" behind some common scams, check with the American Association of Home-Based Businesses or The Federal Trade Commission.

(See: Junk Mail)

Self-Conscious

Being embarrassed, insecure, or unsure about your-self will happen at various times within a person's life span. Some people live with self-consciousness on a daily basis, whether going to work, school, or just walking down the street. We all have a bit of self-conscious discomfort at some time or another. If we feel that someone is staring at us too long, we will probably feel self-conscious and a bit awkward and irritated.

Life is full of so many kinds of emotions. The best thing we can do to get comfortable in our own skin is, "**embrace**" all of the different sensations that we have. Others are feeling the same things too. You are not alone! Don't take your imperfections so seriously, no one is perfect. Famous actors, entertainers and successful politicians all have something that they are self-conscious about. The best thing to do is work on what ever it is that you are self-conscious about.

Then say, I am ok with it now. I can accept not being perfect, no one is! Some people spend a lot of energy just to get a "kick" out of making others feel insecure about themselves. Just remember, they also have "something" that they are self-conscious about too. Never exhaust yourself or waste energy on someone else's negative vibes.

So work on improving whatever it is that makes you feel self-conscious. Then pat yourself on the back and accept your gradual improvements. You will eventually find that comfort level in yourself to say; *I am not perfect and I have improved this flaw or have made peace with it, and I will not let it bother me any more!* (See: Confidence)

Self-Expression

Where would the world be with out "Self- Expression?" Sometimes we want to express ourselves because we have a strong urge to be recognized for our own individuality. We want to stand out from the crowd and say I am unique . . . which is fine to a degree. Self expression can take on many different forms, from unusual hair, tattooed skin, odd clothing and an unruly attitude. Although each generation has their own ways of expressing themselves, some are a little more extreme than others.

But remember, if your "Self-Expression" leaves a "permanent" mark on your mind or body, this will be something you will have to live with even after you have proven your point to the world. Some self expressions lead to permanent damage and some don't. Remember that you are young and you will go through many stages in your life as you grow and mature. About every seven to ten years - you will evolve into something a little different than before; hopefully a new and improved version of the former. So, be careful in how you express yourself. Stop and think . . . ten years from now, is this demonstration of self-expression going to hurt my reputation, body, spirit, or my self-esteem? You make the call, after all you're the only one who can.

Never choose a type of "self-expression" just to upset or embarrass someone. Make sure it's positive in your eye sight and the self-expression is mainly coming from inside of "you" and not someone else. Never follow someone else's idea of self-expression if you are not one-hundred percent comfortable with it.

Setting Goals

Everyone should have goals that they have set for themselves and a process of how to achieve them. You should have "short term goals" and "long term goals." Although your long range goals may change, it is important that you at least have a road map to start your life. If you are just floating around in life, you just might end up nowhere.

Every successful person in life has made setting goals a priority. They know they must carefully plan a road map from "A" to "Z" and must not indulge in *"negative opportunities"* that will interrupt their goals. Start by typing out your "short rang goals" and "long range goals" and put them where you can review them every week. This will help you to "*keep your eye on the prize.*" Consider mailing a copy to your parents or someone you confide in so they can remind you to stay focused. Put blank squares in front of each short range goal so you can check them off when you have accomplished that particular goal. You can also do the same for the things you need to complete on a weekly basis. It is a good feeling to be able to check-off the box that indicates you have completed this specific goal.

Never spend too much time discussing your goals with insignificant people, or should I say "people who don't believe you are capable." Only share your intended goals with those who are interested in seeing you succeed and are willing to support you either morally, emotionally or economically. To keep from losing your focus and ambition, always surround yourself with people that are trying to accomplish and excel; spend less time around those with no realistic aspirations.

(See: Loneliness)

Sexual Exploitation

Sexual exploitation is on the rise in the USA. There are thousands of teenagers, female and male, tricked into the dark underworld of prostitution.

You may be approached by an older attractive female or male telling you how you can "make money" by modeling for them. They will tell you how beautiful and attractive you are and compliment you on one of your most attractive features like you hair, eyes, skin or height. Then they will invite you to meet them someplace to get your, hair, makeup or nails done before your photo-shoot. They may even give you a little money just to suck you in further to make you feel obligated. Then when you are ready for your photo-shoot they will want you to remove certain pieces of clothing.

Their objective is to have nude photos of you and to eventually get you to have sex with their clients. They may give you alcohol or drugs before you walk into the so-called photo shoot area. If you go along with it, they will keep some or all of the money their clients gave them for having sex with you and give you excuses why they should "hold on to your money" for you.

Make no mistake about it . . . if you fall for this —then you are letting them pimp you! If you continue to trust them, they may kidnap you and keep you drugged then pass you on to the next Pimp when they are done with you. Using a fake passport, you could be transported to another country and never know where you are for months at a time. They will control your environment and prevent you from contacting anyone that could possibly help you. They will only let you be around other sick and perverted people who are just like them.

Young female teenagers are their primarily target between the age of 14 and 18 as well as young gullible teenage males. This "game" has been around since man has walked the face of this earth, and more and more sex predators are making their way to the United States each year. Also; getting tricked into the pornography business works basically the same way, beware of offers like;

"You Can Make a Lot of Money." This phrase has "turned-out" more teens into the prostitution and pornography world than any other con phrase around!

Usually, "Fast Money" is not good money!

Remember, never trust anyone who approaches you and offers you a deal for becoming a "Model" unless they are a recruiter from an established agency. If they are legitimate, they won't mind if you bring your parents or an older person along for the interview. Make sure you get their business card and an address where you can contact them. And if you should decide to investigate their offer, be sure to give this information to someone you know and "trust," but you should never go alone.

Agreeing to do anything for $$$ is Not a good way to start your life.

Set your boundaries NOW using the morals that you know are practical, and don't get tricked into crossing the boundaries you have set for yourself. (See: Modeling)

Sleep Deprivation

Face it, a lack of sleep contributes to: thousands of automobile accidents, ineffectiveness on the job, daily irritability and road rage just to name a few. Not getting enough sleep slows down your reflexes, distorts your judgment and basically impairs your brains capacity to think fast and logically. By getting adequate rest, your body has a chance to refurbish brain chemicals, restore hormone balance and strengthen your immune system.

Because you are young you may think that you require less sleep and feel you can function normally on about 4 hours of sound sleep. Some young people boast about not getting any sleep for 48 hours or more. But this damages the body because the body needs rest to replenish itself and to fight off potential infections. Some statistics say that teenagers need about 9 hours per day of sleep and adults need 7 to 8 hours or less.

Obviously our bodies were not designed to act like machines . . . just oil and gas us up and we're good to go. We were created with an internal clock inside of us for a reason, just as the day and night was created for a reason. If you ignore the human element that was built into your body, you will eventually cause incredible damage to your body. Cells will not get adequately rebuilt, and your immune system will suffer making you more susceptible to disease.

The chemicals in the brain that are affected when you sleep are:

- *Serotonin* -- which affects mood, sleep and appetite.
- *Nor epinephrine* -- which affects blood pressure and metabolism.
- *Adenosine* -- which affects the heart and circulatory system.

Anti-depressants and caffeine interfere with the brain's chemical activity. And taking sleeping pills over a period of time can become additive.

Falling asleep with the television on doesn't allow you to get proper sleep. Your subconscious mind will still tune-in to the sounds coming from the television. A quiet room puts the mind at rest and allows for a deeper sleep.

If you are having trouble sleeping, see a sleep specialist for advice.

(See: Drugs & Driving)

STD's

(Sexually Transmitted Diseases)

By now you probably know that STD's stand for Sexually Transmitted Diseases and once called Venereal Diseases. They are transferred by intercourse. They were given the name STD's because there are so many diseases transmitted through sex. STD's can be transmitted through contact with the sexual organs in other ways other than vaginal intercourse. STD bacteria can also be contracted during oral sex and anal sex. Condoms can help prevent you from getting infected, but they are not guaranteed to completely protect you.

Having sex with different people makes you more likely to contract a STD. Therefore you should limit your sexual activity to one person. Most STD's are curable however, many people don't know that they are a carrier. Not all STD's show signs that let you know you are infected. Some STD's in males or females may be "silent" having no noticeable symptoms and can be transported for years without the carrier ever knowing it. An STD roaming around in your body for months or years can contribute to a break-down in your immune system and possibly contribute to other severe ailments within your body.

For some reason, some people won't get "properly" tested even after being informed by a partner that they may be infected. Having no visible or physical symptoms is not an effective measure of whether or not you are infected. Don't stay in denial if someone tells you that you may be infected, get properly tested. Remember, all sexually active parties or partners "must" be treated to kill the disease. Also, if you are pregnant, any STD could be life threatening to an unborn child.

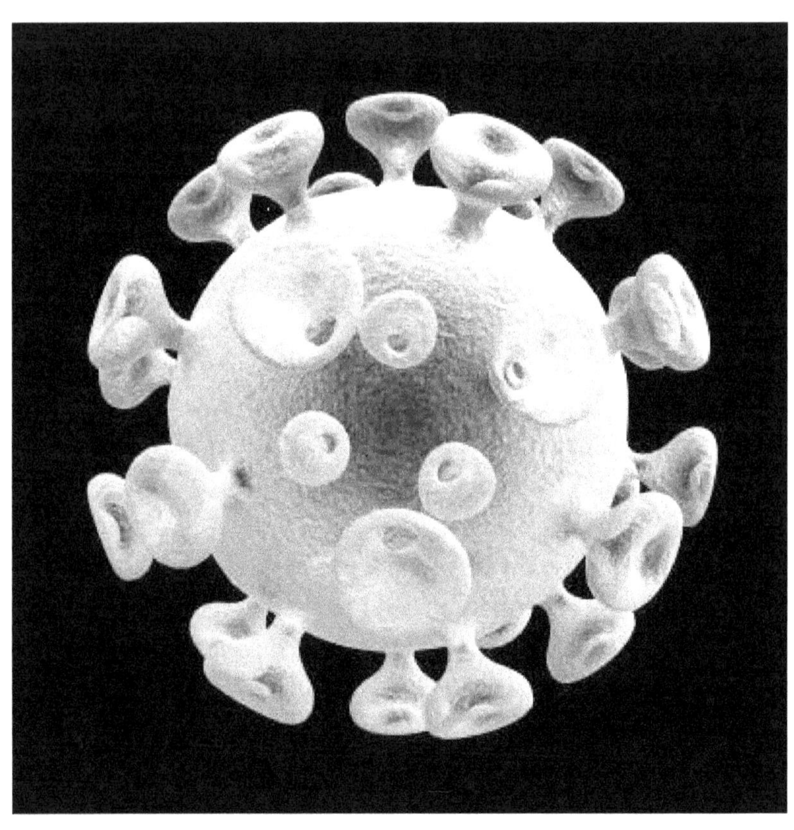

HIV-AIDS are **Incurable and Fatal**, you may have it and not know it.

Many STD's are treated with Antibiotics such as; Axithromycin, Doxycycline, Flagyl, or Metrotrazinol. However some people are allergic to antibiotics and their doctors will prescribe a similar medicine that is safe for them.

<u>Here's a list of some common STD's</u>

Chlamydia
Trichomoniasis
ScabiesVaginal Yeast Infection
Chancroid
Gonorrhea
AID's and HIV
Syphillis
Pelvic Inflammatory Disease
Candidacies
Genital Warts/Herpes HPV
Pubic Lice
Bacterial Vaginosis

<u>Facts:</u>

- Hepatitis A and B are the only STD's that can be prevented with a vaccine.
- HPV can lead to cervical cancer in women.
- An untreated STD can lead to tubal damage caused by PID which can lead to infertility.
- Hepatitus B (HBV) infections can be transferred sexually and can cause chronic liver disease or liver cancer.
- Some strains or gonorrhea are resistant to treatment.
- Herpes (HSV-2), Genital Human Papillomavirus HPV, and Hepatitis B are all incurable.
- HIV-AIDS are **Incurable and Fatal**, you may have it and not know it.

Remember:

When taking antibiotics, the proper Antibiotic should be taken for the specific infectious bacteria. The dosage should also be effective enough to <u>kill all</u> of the infectious bacteria, otherwise it will mutate into a stronger "harder to kill" bacteria. For this reason it is important to take all of the medicine that your doctor prescribes for you.

Because antibiotics work by killing off "all" bacteria in the body—both good and bad, some say acidophilus, should be taken after you have being on antibiotics to restore good bacteria levels within the body. Most yogurts contains live active cultures of Acidophilus, L.Bulgaricus, and Bifidus, which helps rebuild good bacteria in the body. Acidophilis capsals can be bought from most Herb stores in the refrigerated section.

Being promiscuous puts you at a greater risk for catching an STD.

Other Contagious transmitted Diseases

-**Legionnaires:** A form of bacterial pneumonia discovered about 30 years ago and spread mainly in water droplets through air conditioning.

-**Tuberculosis:** An infectious bacterial disease characterized by the growth of tubercles in the tissues, especially the lungs.

-**Staphylococcus:** "Staff" Infections: A parasitic bacteria that can cause boils and blood poisoning infections. In many cases the antibiotic "Duricef" has been known to kill this bacterium.

Tools

Minor Home Improvement

Being able to "repair" a few things around the house will save you time and money. Some tools are self-explanatory and others need a little more instruction. It doesn't matter whether you are male or female; you should know how to do some basic home improvements. Sooner or later you will own a house, probably within the next six to eight years. And having a little knowledge in home repairs will definitely be a big help.

So knowing how to use certain tools are important, even if you are still living in an apartment. Take a course in "Home Improvement" so you will know how to handle minor repairs before purchasing your home. This can save you thousands in a long run.

You should recognize and learn the proper uses for:

> A hammer, hand saw, circular saw, drill, molly bolt, toggle bolt, machine screw, nut, washer, lock washer, wood screw, brad, miter box, channel locks, pliers, Phillips screw driver, flat head screw driver, putty knife, wood chisel and wood putty.

Travel

Traveling can be exciting especially when visiting other countries. However, be especially careful when visiting other countries. Do a little internet research on the city you plan to visit and find out which areas are tourist sites and which ones are the native regions. Find out what areas are considered dangerous, and which areas are poverty stricken. You wouldn't want to be visiting a poor area all dressed up and looking out of place or you may as well carry a big "Flag" announcing that you are a "Tourist." For some natives, Tourists are often targets for con-artist or thieves. Of course some places it doesn't matter how you dress, you will be recognized immediately by your ethnicity.

But still, research what is common and what is permitted for the city you intend to visit. Be informed on the style of dress -to the language and mannerism that is acceptable by your age group. It is always best to take someone with you when traveling; preferably someone you know. Also you might consider contacting a pin pal several months before you go, depending on where you are going. But still you can't always trust a pin pal, you don't really know them either. Always be careful about drinking the water and eating the food in another country. Both water and food can be full of "bad bacteria" and "unfriendly parasites" that can make you extremely sick or even kill you. Research the internet or ask your doctor about certain herbs or medicines you should take along with you.

Stay in contact with someone at home on a regular basis (daily) and let them know where you are. If calling is inconvenient, then use e-mail or text-messaging. You can also drop them daily postcard about your activities. Before you leave on your trip, create some kind of a "code word" that indicates you might be in danger; tell two people who you might contact what the code word(s) are.

Remember it's best to travel with someone you know. As a young adult you are vulnerable prey to the shady talents of the undermining con-artist. They are savvy in their persuasion and trickery. They would love to trick you out of your money for something worthless. Or even worst, drug you and kidnap you then maybe sexually abuse you or get you caught up in a sex-slave ring that you could never escape from. There are a lot of thing going on in the world that your parents have not told you about, and some of your parents aren't even aware that such things exists. But, your parents are always telling you to be cautious of strangers because they know that wickedness exists in this world.

When you are traveling, no need to tell every stranger where you are staying for the night or how long you are going to be visiting etc.. Nor do they need to know everything about you. If a stranger is asking you too many questions . . . "flip the script" and start asking "them" questions. Ask them about their country, their politics, their religion, schools, and their travels. Never tell strangers too much about yourself. You are the vulnerable one in their country. Be in control at all times, don't drink too much, never accept drinks from strangers and never leave a stranger to guard your drink. Never accept a ride in their vehicle unless you know for a FACT that it's safe. Never put yourself in a compromising position where you feel you owe them something.

No matter how smart you are; it is always harder to out-smart someone on their own turf. Stay safe, keep a low profile and stay out of trouble. Getting into trouble in a foreign country could land you in prison; essentially, all "who you know" contacts end and the waters edge. Remember the laws change from country to country and stealing an apple could get you five years depending on the country. Believe it!

Even while traveling within the United States, remember take the same precautions. Criminals reside any and everywhere. Never give them enough information to take advantage of you. And don't let someone cause you to make a foolish agreement on the spot. Don't accept rides, visit strangers homes, or get on their boats, unless you are with several of your friends and you feel there is no potential threat. Weigh the probability of you being able to escape if you had to. Ask yourself if the likelihood of you protecting yourself is "great" or is it "small?"

Uncomfortable Situations

Every so often in life, you will encounter an uncomfortable situation. You may find yourself in a predicament purely by accident and sometimes you may have helped create the situation yourself. Non-the-less, you will be confronted with several uncomfortable situations. Never confuse an "*uncomfortable situation*" with a "*dangerous situation*." The best way to handle an "uncomfortable" situation is with decency. One way of handling an uncomfortable situation is to try and think of someone who you have a great deal of respect for; then act like you think they would act in such a situation. Remember it is usually better to say too little than too much. A quick exit could be an easy answer but sometimes you may have to ride it out.

Although the nature of the situation will no doubt bother you for a few days, you will eventually forget about it. Humans have a tendency to replay certain situations over and over in their heads shortly after something has happened but as time goes by you will think about it a lot less. Use your uncomfortable experiences as lessons learned in life. Also, consider how you could have avoided it or how it has strengthened the core of your character. Many times an uncomfortable situation could be avoided by planning ahead.

(See: Self-Conscious)

Wounded Hearts

If you have broken up with that special person in your life you may feel hurt, angry and confused because you won't be sharing your time with them anymore. They may have been all that you have known for the past few years or so. This is truly a delicate time in your life. You are hit with all kinds of experiences all at once. You think your whole world is crashing in on you. Not one, not two, but three things hitting you all at once! You feel overwhelmed having to deal with so much at such a young age. All the fun of your childhood years dance around you, and you now wish for the carefree life you once had. But you know those days are pretty much gone and people are expecting things of you. You have to be responsible now . . . . You want to hold your head high and ignore all your pain from childhood to the present moment; but it haunts you all at once.

Have HOPE! There will be happy days again, believe it! Just ask anyone over "forty" what has life been like for them. Most of their stories will pretty much be the same. The strong take the lows with "dignity" because they know it won't last forever. When you hit those lows, surround yourself with "trusting" friends, not to sound like a song but . . . "*that's what friends are for*." For good times and bad, just remember that you will sometimes need to be there for them too. And most likely you will go through a few relationships before finding the right companion for you.

After each breakup . . .
you will hurt. You will always feel that you will never find another person that you will like as much as the last boyfriend or girlfriend . . . but, you will. Believe it or not, there is actually more than one person in this world for you. Just stay strong, cry

a few tears, and write a few letters. Then sit down and really think about "what kind" of person you will look for in your next relationship. Look at every aspect of yourself, your personality, your integrity, your communication. You may need to work on a few things to help you become a better person. Improve on those areas that you are lacking in.

Before you enter into another relationship, consider what kind of person you are comfortable being around, and what kind you are uneasy being around. But still, even if you do find that ideal mate, remember humans will keep changing, and there is no guarantee that someone's feelings will stay the same all of their life. Nothing is permanent in life.

Yoke: A symbol of oppression, to link together, unite, servitude, something that binds bond or ties as in marriage.

"Most people won't wind up with the first love of their life anyway. Most go on to meet and get to know other people before they decide to settle down. That's just the way life goes . . . You may feel like your world has come to an end when your partner leaves you, but it's only a temporary feeling. Time will heal your pain. You cannot make someone love you, nor can you make someone fall back in Love with you. Just let it go . . . and move on. Sulk for a few weeks or a few months and get over it!
*'A man and a woman must be **equally yoked**' to make a relationship lasts. You were born into this world alone and not attached to anyone. And if you feel like part of you is missing without that particular person; then you are missing your whole purpose in life. In "Life" you will travel many roads, you will climb a few mountains, pass through deep valleys and cross many streams. It's just part of living . . .*

And NO, you won't be happy all the time. Don't be devastated when things don't go "YOUR" way. Never be that selfish. You are not the God, the director or even the leader of anyone else's life. Everyone has a mission and a purpose in life and you won't know what yours is until you are on the right path

Be Strong, and remember, "Time" heals all wounds.

A Note to Young Ladies:

While you are young (under 24) your must be very careful when considering to date an older man. Some older men seek out young females because they want someone that they can control. They feel they must have someone who relies on them and look up to them. They can also be the "most dangerous" if you are the one who wants to end the relationship. Look it up on the internet; "brutally attacked women in relationships." When men get angry over a woman they are more likely to become enraged and violent more often then women do. Never get caught up in the intrigue of an older man at this early stage in your life; it is too easy for you to get manipulated and abused. Then, if you want to change you mind about dating them they can make your life a living hell. Be very very careful in how you terminate a relationship; always leave them with their pride in tact. And if you hear this phrase--, "if I can't have you, then no one else will," You are in imminent danger and you should be apprehensive. Protect yourself!. Remember a restraining order is merely a piece of paper and won't stop a maniac that wants to do you bodily harm. "Pray" for them, and you. The grave yards are full of women who had "restraining orders" against their attackers. Contact one of the women against violence groups.

Never submit to relying on just anyone for your needs. Focus on your career and your future and work hard for the things that "you" desire in life. It won't always be easy, but the rewards will be worth all the effort, eventually.

No matter what career you decide to pursue, it is going to take some perseverance and dedication. You will need to focus, but mostly, you must sacrifice. In order to achieve your dreams you must resist or limit the time you would spend: partying, daydreaming, having love affairs, using mind altering substances and so forth. There will be plenty of time for fun once you have achieved your goals.

Focus, Focus, Focus. If you let yourself yield to the feel good additions that will surely temp you, you will never succeed in fulfilling your dreams. Frankly speaking . . . there is a time for everything, and if you spend too much time "playing" and not preparing for your future . . . you will not have much of a future! The older you get, the quicker the years will fly.

Never let past memories or people in your past misdirect or confuse you. Their insecurities and doubts can cause you many wasted years. Always consider good advice, but "you" must make the ultimate decision. Never try to prove anything to anyone but yourself. This is the time to set a plan for life, but have a back-up plan too. Make the best of your talents and stick with the things that interest you. The sooner you figure out what your strengths and weaknesses are, the better it will be for you. You must use your intellect, intuition, wisdom and courage to make the right decisions in your life. It will get tough at times, but stay optimistic. Surrender your actions to positive energy and add that to the lessons and instructions that your parents generously gave you; then you should be well on you way to living your dreams.

Remember, *never be afraid of change.* Things change and people change, how mundane it would be if people did not grow and evolve from one decade to the next. Just think if we hadn't change since the 1500 century we would still be stuck in medieval times. How horrific that would be? When one door closes, another opens, when one chapter in life ends another begins, usually better. But you help determine the outcome by what you do and how you accept change!

Always be moral and ethical in your personal and business endeavors or dealing with people. Be honest and considerate, yet strong and tenacious. Have courage. There are lots of lessons to learn throughout your entire life. Pray for yourself and others; ask for knowledge, blessings and forgiveness. Use whatever adversity that comes your way to drive and propel you to a more virtuous level. And when searching for answers, always go "directly" to the correct source. These are the "tools for life," take care of you body, your mind and your spirit; they are all connected, and if one is ill, the other will suffer.

When you are Driving

- Talking on the cell-phone while driving is NOT a good idea, pull over and have that conversation.

- Blast the music with the windows rolled up if you want—but remember you can not hear other car horns, Police, Fire or Ambulance sirens. Prevent an accident by keeping your music at a medium and a window slightly open.

- Waiting a few minutes to fiddle with the radio could make all the difference in getting to your destination safely.

- Don't assume; because someone has their turn signal on that they will actually turn. They may not know their signal is on.

- Changing lanes slowly instead of rapidly is best most of the time.

- Try not to ride in a cluster of cars on the interstate, and try not to get "boxed in" by big rigs.

- When traveling at 60mph, you should be at least 6 car lengths away from the car in front of you.

- Auto Insurance is "Mandatory," it is not an option, and it is illegal to drive a vehicle without it. Make sure you have insurance before driving a vehicle.

- While stopping, do not block driveways or intersections.

- Driving is not a video game, but just the same, objects or vehicles may come at you unexpectedly. Anticipate several possibilities that can cause an accident.

- When stopping behind a vehicle, always stop at a distance where you can see the bottom of the tires of the vehicle in front of you; that way you can go around them if necessary.

- No matter how much "something" is tempting you to look off the road, remember, taking your eyes off the road may not be worth the two second glance if you wind up having an accident.

- When necessary, pull off the road as far as possible. Would you rather be hit by a speeding car or deal with a bug or snake in the grass? Thousands of accidents happen every year when people don't pull off the road far enough.

- Have someone show you how to change a tire. Never change a tire in a area that is too close to the road. A damaged rim is replaceable, your life is not.

- Never drive when you are sleepy, your "reaction time" is so much slower.

- Headlights should be <u>on</u> from sun-down to sun-up. When it's dusty or dark out, headlights help other vehicles see you and help you to see them.

- Vehicles slide and lose control when there is; sand, water, oil, gravel, black ice or clear ice on the road. Anything that is between your tires and the pavement can cause you to slide and lose control of your vehicle.

- Putting your hazard lights on when traffic suddenly slows down may prevent someone from running into the rear end of your vehicle.

- You should never drive when you are extremely emotional or distracted; like after an argument or being told someone dear to you has just died.

- If you can't see a trucks mirrors, it means—they can not see your vehicle either. Try to avoid passing large trucks on the right.

- A flashing yellow light means "slow down" and proceed with caution. A flashing red light means "stop" at the intersection and proceed with caution. HOWEVER, if all of traffic is stopping at the flashing yellow, you probably should do the same.

- Always put on your seat-belt and tell your passengers to buckle-up too. Tell them you might have to put two feet on the brake peddle; that usually gets them to buckle up.

More Stuff to Think About . . .

Remember, you have a right to VOTE, and you have a right to set back and let everyone else make up laws for you to obey. Be a part of your future and vote. Consider the repercussions of voting "for" or "against" war. Are a Republican, Democrat or Independent?

-"*Don't count your chickens before they hatch*" is an old saying. Remember it before doing something merely based on the possibility of something happening. Like . . . spending money you don't have yet. If it is not in your hand or in your bank account, then—you do not have it! Always base your life on "Actual" substance and not weak possibilities.

-Never leave your drink unguarded or with anyone you do not trust completely; someone could drop rohypnol in it, which is a drug that affects memory but it can kill you too. There is another drug with similar effects, however it makes the female sterile and she will **never** be able to conceive. Don't be a victim of a dirty trick.

-Stay focused in life; always strive to prevail over evil.

-Don't get caught-up in watching too much television, remember you are simply watching others make money.

-Never go to sleep when you are cooking—could cause a fire. Keep a working smoke detector on the ceiling. And buy a small fire extinguisher.

-Never go to sleep with space heaters on, they could cause a fire. Buy an electric blanket or electric mattress pad.

-The odds of getting away with a major crime holds the same probability of winning a major lottery; about one in 1.2 billion. "Always do the Right Thing"

-Always have some kind of Identification with you.

-Tame your bad thoughts and fight your demons. Don't invite evil into your life.

-Never deliberately antagonize someone, you don't know what their limitations are or when they may SNAP!

-Find out what weaknesses "You" have, then work on eliminating them and improving on your strengths.

-Drink plenty of spring water or distilled water daily to flush out toxins in your body. Sip water throughout the day. It benefits the body less if you guzzle several glass-fulls at one time.

-An old wise saying to live by goes like this . . . "God grant me the serenity to "accept" the things I cannot change, the "courage" to change the things I can, and the "wisdom" to know the difference."

-It is illegal to write a check knowing that it will bounce because there is not enough money in the bank to cover it. You might be charged with a felony if charges are brought against you.

-Watch the **News** at least 3 times a week to see what's going on in the world and to get information that could be important, like: updates on contaminated food, changes in laws, or dangerous criminals in your area.

-"*Study Volunteers Needed.*" A newspaper ad like this may sound interesting, but before you go and sign-up as a "test subject" for some "New Medication," first consider the future side effects that could haunt your body for the rest of your life.

-Before buying a used or pre-owned vehicle, check the vehicle history by using the Vehicle Identification Number (VIN). You can find out if the car has been wrecked or reported stolen. Go to: www.dmv.org or http://www.AutoTrader.com And don't buy a car with a "Salvaged Title" look at the title before any money exchanges hands.

- Unless you own a company, you probably should not "lease purchase" a vehicle. Research the negative factors in "leasing" a vehicle.

-You will face additional felony charges if you have illegal drugs or unsecured weapons in your home and children are present. Don't be reckless, a child is precious, don't put them in harms way.

-If you want to sell products on the street or out of your car you will need a "peddler's license."

-If you want to question people on the streets to find out their opinion or idea for a plan for discussion, you will need a "canvasser's license."

-To hand out information or when going door to door soliciting products or services, you may need a "solicitors license."

-Sex . . . you had better ask to see "Identification" before you get involved with someone if you are not positive about their age. Whether you are male or female, you don't want to wind up in court battling a guilty plea to having sex or giving alcohol to a minor who is only a year or two younger than you. Believe it or not, some states hold stiffer penalties for oral sex than for any other kinds. See the case with Genarlow Wilson at: www.WilsonAppeal.com

-Student Loans and IRS debts are with you until you pay them off. IRS debt can sometimes be reduced or negotiated with an "Offer in Compromise" agreement.

-A credit report is how Lending Institutions evaluate your character.

-When buying a home, be aware of "Covenants" on the land. Most land or real estate have covenants. These are what you *can* or *can not* do to your property . . . Most Subdivisions and Condominiums have covenants and association fees. Ask any Real Estate agent about it.

-Get counseling for childhood anger and pain issues. Do not bring your anger and frustration into your relationship.

-Christians believe in living by the Ten Commandments 1, 2, 3, 4, 5, 6, 7, 8, 9, 10. They are basic and practical guidelines for life.

-Nutrition: Taking acidophilus found in Yogurt is said to help restore good bacteria in the body after taking antibiotics.

-Detox your body at least every other month. Visit your local Herbal Health food store.

-If you pay $600.00 rent for 7 years, you will have invested $50,400 in someone else's real estate.

- Try not to visit friends or family members so much that you wear-out your welcome; pay attention to others attitude. Even if asked; most people will not say they want you to leave or that they don't want you to come over. Instead they might make up excuses why they won't be at home. Never over extend your welcome or infringe on others space, know when it's time to leave. People should be happy to see you coming—not happy to see you leaving!

-Take care of your feet. You can cause tremendous damage to your feet by wearing shoes that hurt. Ouch!

-Eating: It's not necessary for you to clean your plate. Leaving food on you plate is not a sin, but you should try not to put more on your plate than you can eat.

-Sometimes you must Sacrifice—Your Wants— for Your Needs.

-The top two causes of death for young adults are: Vehicle Accidents and Aids. Live Safe!

-If you get in trouble with the law remember you have a constitutional right to a Jury trial. Watch the Movie "Justice" with Roger Smith and Monica Calhoun.

Words to Know

Acronym: A word formed by using the first initial of other words.

Acute: Sharp or severe. Very serious or critical. (disease or illness)

Altruistic: Showing unselfish concern for the welfare of others.

Amenity: Pleasantness as a result from agreeable conditions.

Arbor: A shady canopy usually made of wood sometimes covered with plants.

Awe: A feeling of deep respect.

Barter: To trade and exchange goods instead of using money. Haggle or bargain with.

Bellows: A device having a bag with two handles and used for blowing air into a fire.

Benevolent: Kindness and a desire to help others. Producing good.

Bureaucracy: Government Administrators that hinder progress because of routine "red tape."

Cajole: To persuade, coax, or influence by using gentle flattery or promises.

Celibate: Abstaining from sexual relations.

Chauvinistic: A person with a prejudiced loyalty to a particular gender or cause.

Coerced: Persuaded to do something, threatened or forced.

Concur: To agree with.

Contiguous: Sharing a common border as in touching or together in sequence.

Conviction: To firmly commit to a belief or opinion about something.

Covenants: Formal agreement, contracts/pledges.

Depreciate: Reduce or go down in value over a period of time.

Despise: To feel someone or something is worthless or to look down on.

Disdain: Feeling like someone is unworthy of one's respect.

Duress: Violence or treats used to persuade or coerce someone to do something.

Eccentric: Slightly strange and unconventional.

Ecstatic: Emotional feeling of ecstasy, joyfulness, or excitement.

Embezzlement: Stealing or misappropriate money that was entrusted to you.

Endeavor: An earnest attempt or effort to achieve something.

Exile: To be barred from one's native country.

Facetious: Not to be taken literally or seriously more so to be clever or humorous.

Firmament: A literary term referring to the heavens and the sky.
Fruition: Fulfilling a plan or achieving something one has tried to do.
Genre: A class of artistic technique. A particular style such as expressing yourself in writing.
Halitosis: Unpleasant or bad smelling breath.
Hermaphrodite: A person or animal having both female and male sex organs.
Heterosexual: Being sexually attracted to the opposite sex.
Homophobia: An extreme or irrational dislike for homosexuals or homosexuality.
Homophone: Two words pronounced the same way but with different meaning or spelling or both. beat/beet
Idiosyncrasies: Having peculiar behavior or way of thinking.
Impala: A southern and East Africa antelope with horns.
Imperative: Essential or urgent thing of vital importance.
Indigo: A dark blue dye obtained from a tropical plant that looks blue and violet.
Intuition: The ability to know something automatically without conscious explanation.

Kosher: To satisfy requirements of Jewish law regarding the preparation of food.

Left wing: The radical or liberal factor in a political party.

Loquacious: Full of trivial conversation, excessive talkativeness.

Masochistic: To get pleasure from your own pain or humiliation.

Metaphysic: Philosophy and abstract concepts regarding knowledge and truth.

Mezzanine: A large balcony area of a building.

Millennium: A time period of 1000 years.

Myopia: Short-sightedness or lacking intellectual insight.

Net income: Income that is left after taxes has been taken out.

Notary: A person who is authorized to certify certain legal documents like contracts or deeds.

Oblivious: Not being aware of what is happening around you.

Organic: Foods not grown with chemical fertilizers.

Ottoman: A low stool for a seated person to rest their feet on.

Pedophile: An adult who is sexually attracted to children.

Philanthropy: Concern for human beings, donating to organizations and institutions.

Platonic: Friendship and affection but no sexual relations.

Proficient: Competent and skilled.

Promiscuous: Loose licentious behavior, having sex with several different people.

Pyromania: An irrational desire for setting things on fire.

Quarry: An open excavation in the earth that stones or slate are extracted from.

Reciprocate: To respond to an action or a gesture with a corresponding gesture or action.

Red Tape: Needless time-consuming operations.

Redundant: Repetition or repeating something such as words or text.

Reparations: To compensate of make amends for a wrong, to repair.

Resilient: Being able to withstand and recover quickly from a difficult situation or condition.

Rhetorical Question: A question asked not for a reply, but mostly to bring about an effect.

Salmonella: A bacteria that occurs in the stomach and can cause food poisoning.

Serendipity: The ability to make fortunate discoveries on mere accident.

Status quo: The current or present state of affairs.
Suffice: To be: sufficient, enough, or adequate.
Vicarious: A secondhand experience, through feelings or actions of someone else.
Vindicate: To clear from an accusation.
Wainscot: The wooden paneling on the lower part of the walls of a room, usually painted.
Zeal: Having great energy and enthusiasm for something.

(Remember, many words have more than one meaning.)

Helpful Websites

Search box: "Outrageous Injustice" Find: Blogs, Forums and Message boards, on people who are convicted of "outrageous crimes" from old laws.

Interesting discussions on Talk Radio at: www.dysontalk.net www.RushLimbaugh.com, or www.ArmstrongWilliams.com with Sam Greenfield. Go to these web-sites to find the radio stations "dial" in your city or listen from your computer.

They discuss crucial issues of; food safety, industrial agriculture, genetic engineering, children's health etc. at: www.organicconsumers.org

"The Slow Poisoning of America" Health and knowledge; information on the poisons in our food and water that's destroying our lives." www.spofamerica.com

Health; what can you eat to eliminate fat? www.just-think-it.com

Lots of good information at this site; don't let the name fool you. http://www.worldalmanacforkids.com

Find very interesting books to read here at the: Young Adult Library Services Association. http://www.ala.org/yalsa

Find books written by Teens. They offer a variety of books and services for young adults. www.Reads4teens.org www.carmel.lib.in.us/default.htm

Site focus: Alcohol and Teen Drinking.
http://www.focusas.com/Alcohol.html

Career or Job Salary Guide at: http://www.CourseAdvisor.com, http://www.PayScale.com and, http://www.JobsOnline.net

Information about product labels, what's really in your food? http://www.truthinlabeling.org

Find biographies about well known people; who were born on your birthday. www.biography.com

Find your Roots. www.AfricanAncestry.com or www.ancestry.com

Notes from your parent(s)...

Write down the goals you plan to accomplish within the next 5 years!

*Date:*____________

www.ingramcontent.com/pod-product-compliance
Lightning Source LLC
LaVergne TN
LVHW050638100826
845148LV00011B/1898

* 9 7 8 0 9 7 6 4 6 1 0 1 2 *